Seek HIM

Seek HIM

Workbook 2

Natasha L. Foreman

D.O.M.E. Life Publishing An Imprint of Foreman & Associates, LLC DOMELifePublishing.com

CONTENTS

Opening Prayer

Acknowledgment

Introduction   4

MONTH FIVE: Surveying Your World

Day 125: Serve God. Period.   6

Day 126: Share Your Testimony Without Expectations   7

Day 127: Don't Be a Scrooge   8

Day 128: You Possess The Power to Heal   9

Day 129: Be a Child of The Light   10

Day 130: It's Your Relationship. Embrace it!   11

Day 131: He Doesn't Need You, How Special Is That?!?   12

Day 132: Walk Like Daniel   13

Day 133: Would Jesus???   14

Day 134: Know No Stranger   15

Day 135: We Are All Tested   16

Day 136: He Is Where You Are   17

Day 137: Stop Judging Others   18

CONTENTS

- Day 138: Deception Strangles — 19
- Day 139: Choose Wisely The Company That You Keep — 20
- Day 140: You Could Lose it All — 21
- Day 141: Rooted in Love — 22
- Day 142: God's Serious, Honor Your Parents — 23
- Day 143: Mold Me — 24
- Day 144: A Woman's Place? — 25
- Day 145: God's Exit Strategy — 26
- Day 146: The Same Spirit — 27
- Day 147: Jesus Is Our Grapevine — 28
- Day 148: God Is All in All — 29
- Day 149: Temptation in Marriage — 30
- Day 150: Getting in God's Way — 31
- Day 151: Obedience — 32
- Day 152: Membership, Ministry, and Mission — 33
- Day 153: What Have You Done For Me Lately? — 34
- Day 154: How Do You Feel About Your Life? — 35

MONTH SIX: CHALLENGING THE STATUS QUO

- Day 155: Grace — 38
- Day 156: Jesus As Our Wayshower — 39
- Day 157: Temptation Costs More Than You Can Afford — 40

CONTENTS

- Day 158: It Isn't About You — 41
- Day 159: Thank God in Advance — 42
- Day 160: Live in Your Situation — 43
- Day 161: Power in Words — 44
- Day 162: God's Wisdom — 45
- Day 163: What Will It Take? — 46
- Day 164: Our Tests — 47
- Day 165: It May Not Be As Soon As You Want — 49
- Day 166: Fight the "Liar" — 50
- Day 167: Pray, Study, and Meditate Daily — 51
- Day 168: No Limits — 52
- Day 169: Good for You — 53
- Day 170: Speak For Others — 54
- Day 171: Imagine Your Life — 55
- Day 172: Clarity — 56
- Day 173: You May Know Him, But Do You Glorify Him? — 57
- Day 174: Truth, Always Be Revealed — 58
- Day 175: May Your Pain Still Be Your Blessing — 59
- Day 176: Rejoice in His Work — 60
- Day 177: God Is the Solution — 61
- Day 178: Endurance — 62

CONTENTS

Day 179: Steer Me Clear   63

Day 180: Impatience   64

Day 181: In God's Sight   65

Day 182: Is This Global Karma?   66

Day 183: Let Hate Motivate You to Love   67

Day 184: Goodness From Within   68

MONTH SEVEN: CHALLENGING THE DISCOMFORT

Day 185: Rethink Christmas   70

Day 186: Don't Test God   71

Day 187: Absolution   72

Day 188: Righteous Like Noah   73

Day 189: Why Not?   74

Day 190: He Heals   75

Day 191: Will You Be The Redeemed?   76

Day 192: Worthy of His Calling   77

Day 193: Don't Be Deceived   78

Day 194: Control Your Heart   79

Day 195: Spiritual Maturity   80

Day 196: Reconciliation to God   81

Day 197: Circumcised in Him   82

Day 198: Be Steadfast   83

CONTENTS

- Day 199: First Adam to Last — 84
- Day 200: Faithful Over The Household — 86
- Day 201: One Flesh in Marriage — 87
- Day 202: Women Builders — 89
- Day 203: A Confident Heart — 90
- Day 204: Selfless Service — 91
- Day 205: Seeing God Everywhere — 92
- Day 206: What Will You Do For Your Friend? — 93
- Day 207: Never Ever Give Up — 94
- Day 208: Fools Make More Fools — 95
- Day 209: Mouth Full Of What? — 96
- Day 210: Setting the Example For Your Household — 97
- Day 211: Your Obligation — 98
- Day 212: Supporting God Is Faith — 99
- Day 213: Death Is No Master — 100
- Day 214: Feed My Sheep — 101

MONTH EIGHT: CHALLENGING THE LIES

- Day 215: Your Lying Words — 104
- Day 216: Hijacking The Church — 105
- Day 217: Charged With a Calling — 106
- Day 218: The Marys' — 107

CONTENTS

Day 219: Bribed to Keep a Lie 108

Day 220: Backstabbers 109

Day 221: Death Didn't Stop Him 110

Day 222: Time to Clean House 111

Day 223: Jesus' RoadShow 112

Day 224: Choose Life 113

Day 225: Rooted In God's Love 114

Day 226: Sabbath Hypocrite 115

Day 227: You Are the Light 116

Day 228: Without Hesitation 117

Day 229: Apart From God 118

Day 230: Value in Your Giving 119

Day 231: Truth Needs No Force 120

Day 232: Only Believe 121

Day 233: Don't Let FOMO Get You Caught Up 122

Day 234: Reach Out in Obedience 123

Day 235: Throw Stones Your Way 124

Day 236: His Faithfulness Endures Forever 125

Day 237: Hope Defined 126

Day 238: Growing in God's Grace 127

Day 239: What Prophecy Is NOT 128

CONTENTS

Day 240: Supplement Faith 129

Day 241: Your Protector Never Sleeps 130

Day 242: Fact-Checking and Truth Speaking 131

Day 243: Death Destroyed 132

Day 244: What Is Most Important in Your Life? 133

GREATER CONTEXT

136

Next Steps 167

NOTES 169
ABOUT THE AUTHOR 171

Copyright © 2021 by Natasha Foreman
D.O.M.E. Life Publishing
Foreman & Associates, LLC
Post Office Box 1912, Mableton, GA 30126

First Edition, 2021

All rights reserved. No part of this book may be reproduced in any manner whatsoever without written permission except in the case of brief quotations embodied in critical articles and reviews.

D.O.M.E. Life Publishing, Imprint of Foreman & Associates, LLC
Books may be purchased in bulk for educational, business, fundraising, or sales promotional use.
For information, please email info@DomeLifePublishing.com

Library of Congress Control Number: 2020917120
ISBN 13:978-1-7355450-5-9
Published in the United States of America

Scripture quotations marked (AMP) are taken from the Amplified Bible, Copyright © 1954, 1958, 1962, 1964, 1965, 1987 by The Lockman Foundation. Used by permission. Scripture quotations taken from the Amplified® Bible (AMPC), Copyright © 1954, 1958, 1962, 1964, 1965, 1987 by The Lockman Foundation Used by permission. www.lockman.org. Scripture quotations marked (ASV) are taken from the American Standard Version, published in 1901 by Thomas Nelson & Sons; public domain. Scripture quotations marked (CEV) are taken from the CONTEMPORARY ENGLISH VERSION, Copyright© 1995 by the American Bible Society. Used by permission. Scripture quotations marked (CSB) have been taken from the Christian Standard Bible®, Copyright © 2017 by Holman Bible Publishers. Used by permission. Christian Standard Bible® and CSB® are federally registered trademarks of Holman Bible Publishers. Scripture quotations marked (CJB) are taken from the COMPLETE JEWISH BIBLE, Copyright© 1998 by David H. Stern. Published by Jewish New Testament Publications, Inc. www.messianicjewish.net. Distributed by Messianic Jewish Resources Int'l. www.messianicjewish.net. All rights reserved. Used by permission. Scripture quotations marked (Dar) are taken from the DARBY BIBLE, published in 1867, 1872, 1884, 1890; public domain. Scripture quotations marked (DRC1752) are taken from the Douay-Rheims Challoner Revision, public domain. Edited by Richard Challoner, 1749-1752, translated by English College at Douai and Rheims. Scripture quotations marked ESV are from the ESV® Bible (The Holy Bible, English Standard Version®), copyright © 2001 by Crossway Bibles, a publishing ministry of Good News Publishers. Used by permission. All rights reserved. Scripture quotations marked HCSB are been taken from the Holman Christian Standard Bible®, Copyright © 1999, 2000, 2002, 2003 by Holman Bible Publishers. Used by permission. Holman Christian Standard Bible®, Holman CSB®, and HCSB® are federally registered trademarks of Holman Bible Publishers. Scripture taken from the Holy Bible: International Standard Version® Release 2.0. Copyright © 1996-2013 by the ISV Foundation. Used by permission of Davidson Press, LLC. ALL RIGHTS RESERVED INTERNATIONALLY. KJV: King James Version Used by Public Domain worldwide with the exception of the United Kingdom. In that regard: Scripture quotations from The Authorized (King James) Version. Rights in the Authorized Version in the United Kingdom are vested in the Crown. Reproduced by permission of the Crown's patentee, Cambridge University Press. Scripture taken from The Message. Copyright Â© 1993, 1994, 1995, 1996, 2000, 2001, 2002. Used by permission of NavPress Publishing Group. Scripture quotations taken from the New American Standard Bible® (NASB), Copyright © 1960, 1962, 1963, 1968, 1971, 1972, 1973, 1975, 1977, 1995 by The Lockman Foundation. Used by permission. www.Lockman.org. Scripture quotations marked (NIV) are taken from the Holy Bible, New International Version®, NIV®. Copyright © 1973, 1978, 1984, 2011 by Biblica, Inc.™ Used by permission of Zondervan. All rights reserved worldwide. www.zondervan.com The "NIV" and "New International Version" are trademarks registered in the United States Patent and Trademark Office by Biblica, Inc.™ Scripture taken from the New King James Version®. Copyright © 1982 by Thomas Nelson. Used by permis-

CONTENTS

sion. All rights reserved. Scripture quotations marked (NLT) are taken from the Holy Bible, New Living Translation, copyright ©1996, 2004, 2015 by Tyndale House Foundation. Used by permission of Tyndale House Publishers, a Division of Tyndale House Ministries, Carol Stream, Illinois 60188. All rights reserved. Scripture taken from The Orthodox Jewish Bible Copyright 2011 by AFI International. All rights reserved. Scripture taken from the Holy Scriptures, Tree of Life Version. Copyright © 2014, 2016 by the Tree of Life Bible Society. Used by permission of the Tree of Life Bible Society.

Opening Prayer

Father, You know what we need and You know that until we choose to surrender fully to You, we will continue to wrestle and struggle with You and Your ways. Guide us, redirect us, restrain us so that we don't walk away too soon and miss the answers before us. There is so much that is in plain sight. There is a great deal that we would know and understand if we only spoke directly with You. For any of Your children reading this, who struggle with hearing Your voice above others, who struggle with coming to You just as they would a human parent or friend—help them to hear and connect with You. Help them to gain a deeper, more intimate relationship with You. Help them to see the beauty of life through Your lens. Help them to break through their spiritual, mental, and physical comfort zones. I praise You, Father, today and each day. Amen.

—Natasha L. Foreman

Acknowledgment

I give God all of the glory for this workbook and the other books in this series. If it weren't for Him none of this would be possible. I humbly submit this workbook to be used as a tool to help with breaking down your walls and pushing past your comfort zone. It's only possible when we ride in the passenger seat next to God. Thank you to everyone who said that a workbook is an added value, and for you, I present this tool.

Introduction

I'm going to keep this short and sweet because I know that you just want to dive right in and get to work. If you're reading this then you most likely already completed *"Seek Him, Volume 1: Testing Your Spiritual Comfort Zone"* and *"Seek Him: Workbook 1"*. If you're shaking your head, no, then you're in for a surprise. This workbook and Seek Him, Volume 2 pick up where Volume 1 and Workbook 1 left off. So if you never read and completed the first two books, I strongly suggest that you do before beginning this next phase. This workbook is designed to lovingly challenge you to go beyond your comfort zone. You can only do that once you first test your limits. So pop over to your local bookstore or jump online and purchase Volume 1 and Workbook 1 to begin testing your comfort zone.

If you're right where you're supposed to be— this is your next level experience, then let me tell you what to expect from this workbook. Over the next four months we will be letting go of more junk we have no business carrying around, releasing even more things into our "For God" containers, and we're going to begin taking an extra step that is tied to gratitude. I will leave it at that, for now. Look at it as a little teaser at what's to come. I have to keep you on your toes, right? There are some free downloads to better assist you at DOMELifePublishing.com, check it out. I hope that they are helpful.

The goal of this workbook is to help us boldly make moves to identify and push past our fears in every area of our life, to surrender to God all of the things we try to fix and control, and seek Him in every situation. We begin Seek Him, Volume 2, and this workbook on Day 125 and conclude on Day 244. Then you will see a section that follows at the end of this workbook. Yes, I brought back the Greater Context chapter, and I'm bringing more weight to challenge what you know and open your eyes and mind to the possibilities. Hopefully, you will refer to the Greater Context chapter more frequently and not just after completing Day 244. You will see that there are certain topics that I revisited from Workbook 1, to provide another layer of information, more detailed and rich. I hope you find it beneficial.

If you did a fast calculation, then maybe you have realized that, unlike the last books, Volume 2 and Workbook 2 are based on 30 calendar days and not 31 days. This should make it easier to navigate through the month-end Go Beyond activities found in Seek Him, Volume 2. I don't want to overwhelm you by having two major readings and upwards of three activities on the last day of a month—which is what we navigated through in Volume 1. With this new approach, there is greater balance. I look forward to taking this journey with you these next four months. If you're ready, I'm ready. Let's do this!

MONTH FIVE: Surveying Your World

Day 125: Serve God. Period.

GO DEEPER!

What will you do today to be of service, in honor of God?

NOTES

Day 126: Share Your Testimony Without Expectations

GO DEEPER!
1. How will you be a blessing to others today?
2. Who will you share today's message with?

NOTES

Day 127: Don't Be a Scrooge

GO DEEPER!

Today's Test: Give money freely to at least three (3) people who are less fortunate than you. Don't question them about what they will use the money for, don't prejudge them, and don't place conditions on the gift. Just give it and bless them. It doesn't matter how much that you give, just give what comes to your heart.

NOTES

Day 128: You Possess The Power to Heal

GO DEEPER!

1. What are you afraid of?
2. What fears or doubts do you have about your relationship with God?
3. Do you feel as though you're worthy of God's love, grace, and blessings? Why?
4. Repeat the affirmations in today's "Speak Your Truth" until you feel empowered. Or until it feels like the load on your shoulders has reduced.
5. Write your fears and doubts on a sheet of paper, and place the paper in the "For God" container [that you created in Seek Him: Workbook 1]. There is a free downloadable sheet at DOMELifePublishing.com that you can also print and use.

NOTES

Day 129: Be a Child of The Light

GO DEEPER!

1. What lies are you telling yourself? Why?
2. What lies have you told others? Why?
3. Have the consequences of those lies been felt by you or them?
4. What lies are you still telling people? Why?
5. What is the worst possible outcome that could result in your lies being uncovered?
6. How does that make you feel?
7. Are you willing to risk exposure by keeping the lie? Why?
8. What cords do you need to cut this year? Why?

Now, recite the affirmations in today's "Speak Your Truth" [in Seek Him, Volume 2]. Are they still accurate? If not, why? What has changed in your heart and mind? Taking into consideration what you have shared in this "Go Deeper" session, recite the "Speak Your Truth" affirmations again. This time, actually speak your truth. Be honest with yourself so that you can begin living an authentic life. Write your "Speak Your Truth" affirmations on a sheet of paper, write today's date, and place it in your "For God" container. You can also use the free downloadable sheets located at DOMELifePublishing.com

NOTES

Day 130: It's Your Relationship. Embrace it!

GO DEEPER!

Spend at least 10 minutes having a conversation with God. You can either start the conversation by repeating today's prayer or saying your own. You can use the affirmations in the "Speak Your Truth" section, to begin the conversation. Whichever approach you like, there's no right or wrong way. Just speak to Him, and then listen. Be sure to pay attention to your feelings and thoughts. Take note of any sights, sounds, and takeaways that you have from the conversation.

NOTES

Day 131: He Doesn't Need You, How Special Is That?!?

GO DEEPER!

1. Take inventory of how your ego and pride get in the way.
2. Knowing this, why do you think that you continue to let this happen?
3. Write a note to God and then add it to your "For God" container.

NOTES

Day 132: Walk Like Daniel

GO DEEPER!

If you are not a student of Daniel's life, learn more about him by reading the book of Daniel in the Bible. There are 12 chapters. Depending on your level of interest, you can either choose the next 12 days or 12 weeks to read each chapter. It's one thing to mention Daniel, in passing, with brief recollections of why he is so highly regarded. It's okay to commit yourself to the "Daniel's Fast" at the beginning of the year when your church urges you to do so. But wouldn't it be better if you knew him more intimately? Well, then read his story.

Take notes on some of the things that stood out most to you when reading about Daniel. In what ways would you like to be more Daniel? Why?

NOTES

Day 133: Would Jesus???

GO DEEPER!

As you journey through your day, be mindful of those moments when God speaks to you. Listen for those moments when He encourages you to be a light in someone else's life. When you hear His calling upon you, stop long enough to help someone else get one step closer to Him.

1. Take note of how you feel/felt doing this?
2. Do you feel awkward or empowered?
3. Do you feel like you are imposing or sharing?
4. Why do you think this way?

NOTES

Day 134: Know No Stranger

GO DEEPER!

Try Something: Ask God to bless every person that you come across. It can be as brief of a request as, "Bless them, Father". At the end of the day, take note of how you felt praying for strangers. Imagine if these same people did the same for you. Reflect upon that. How does it make you feel thinking about that as a reality?

NOTES

Day 135: We Are All Tested

GO DEEPER!

1. What tests or challenges are you facing now?
2. What is your desired outcome?
3. Is it doable?
4. Have you spoken to God about these tests and challenges?
5. What did He say?
6. What does this mean to you?
7. What can you do to make things less complicated?

Add your responses to a sheet of paper, write today's date, and place it in your "For God" container. You can also use the free downloadable sheets located at DOMELifePublishing.com

NOTES

Day 136: He Is Where You Are

GO DEEPER!

1. What cares and concerns would you like to turn over to God?
2. Is there a place where you fear to be? Why?
3. How would you like for God to reassure you?

Share this on a sheet of paper, with today's date, and place it in your "For God" container. You can also use the free downloadable sheets located at DOMELifePublishing.com

NOTES

Day 137: Stop Judging Others

GO DEEPER!

Try Something: Throughout the day today, do not judge others. Don't prejudge them about their appearance, accent, hygiene, or opinions. Don't pass judgment on someone's intelligence, socioeconomic status, or religious beliefs. Don't judge a person's sexual orientation, sexual preferences, food choices, or music preferences.

Note the times when you struggled and gave into judging someone. Why do you think you were quick to judge them? What about them came under the scrutiny of your judgment?

Think of the times when you didn't judge, but you know that in the past you would have. What are your thoughts about this?

Do you think you would be interested in trying this again tomorrow? If yes, challenge yourself to do so. Journal about your judgmental and nonjudgmental moments.

NOTES

Day 138: Deception Strangles

GO DEEPER!

Turn your book to Day 129. Make another attempt at that day's "Go Deeper" session. Take notes about your thoughts and feelings about the exercise.

NOTES

Day 139: Choose Wisely The Company That You Keep

GO DEEPER!

1. List your circle of influence. The list can include your spouse/significant other, your friends, associates, and acquaintances.
2. Which of those individuals do you see as positive and optimistic?
3. How does it feel when you spend time with them?
4. Which individuals make you feel as though you have to be mindful of the energy that you exert with them? Do you consider them energy drainers?
5. Which individuals, can you admit, are negative or drama-magnets?
6. Do you spend a lot of time listening to their stories about how someone offended or harmed them? Does it seem as though drama always finds them?
7. How did you come to know your circle? What made you gravitate to these people?
8. Why did you choose to maintain relationships with them?

NOTES

Day 140: You Could Lose it All

GO DEEPER!

In what ways can you focus on wealth without turning money into your god?

NOTES

Day 141: Rooted in Love

GO DEEPER!

Try Something Today: If you're hurt or upset by someone, try to pause long enough to listen to God on how to handle the situation. That way, you can respond, or not, with love and not hate (or indifference). God may have you respectfully engage or walk away.

At the end of the day, take notes about your successes or failures with today's exercise.

1. How did you feel today trying this exercise?
2. Did it come naturally? Or did you struggle with allowing God to guide you (versus taking the reigns yourself)?
3. How do you feel now, at this very moment?

If you feel comfortable trying this again tomorrow, please do. Revisit this section and repeat steps 2 to 4 above.

NOTES

Day 142: God's Serious, Honor Your Parents

GO DEEPER!

Take some time today to speak to God. Talk to Him about how you would like to forgive your parents for the offenses that they committed. Both real and imagined. Then share with Him the things that you're grateful for because of the role that they played in your life. This could be your conception, birth, and upbringing.

Yes, even if you were adopted, abandoned, abused, or neglected. Attempt to have this conversation with God. Even if this includes questions or statements about your parents' behavior or lifestyle. Speak to Him. Whether you have children or not, how did their parenting style impact yours? You may say, "*But I don't have children*". I would still say, in some ways at some point in your life, you have helped to parent a child. You have served as a mentor or role model. Use that as your frame of reference.

NOTES

Day 143: Mold Me

GO DEEPER!

Try Something Today: Look around at the people that you see in buildings, parking lots, and on the streets. Imagine if they are Jesus. If you struggle with this, consider visualizing them as angels. Remove the image of halos, harps, and wings. Remove the image of bodies with glowing lights cascading around them. God doesn't need the dramatics to place His creations amongst us. We already know that angels could and can transform into human form. You don't know which angels walk amongst you—God's faithful or satan's crew.

At the end of the day, reflect on your experience.

1. Did you struggle with seeing others as Jesus? Why?
2. Could you visualize them as angels, walking amongst us? Why?
3. What if one of those people were Jesus, what did he hear you saying, and what did he see you doing?

Take this in. Process it.

NOTES

Day 144: A Woman's Place?

GO DEEPER!

1. Consider today's Reflection in Seek Him, Volume 2. Now flip to the back of this workbook and go to the GREATER CONTEXT chapter and read what I wrote in the section "Paul's Letter to Church of Corinth: 1 Corinthians 14:26-35".
2. What are your thoughts about today's message and the information shared in GREATER CONTEXT?
3. Why do you agree or disagree with the information that I shared in both books?
4. If religious leaders shared the same information about lines 33-35 that I provided in these books, what would be different in churches? What kind of changes could we see?
5. How could those changes impact communities and the world? How could an embrace of this different way of thinking change laws, politics, and businesses?
6. Write down what you would like to turn over to God, write today's date, and place it in your "For God" container. You can also use the free downloadable sheets located at DOMELifePublishing.com

NOTES

Day 145: God's Exit Strategy

GO DEEPER!

1. Can you tell the difference between God's tests and Satan's temptations? How?
2. At the end of the day, note the various temptations that you were able to resist, or you succumbed to—and reflect on how you feel.
3. What did you do, say, or think to resist the temptation?
4. What happened that caused you to succumb to temptation?
5. What "tests" are you currently working through?
6. Write a prayer to God about the temptations and tests that you are facing, and ask Him for guidance and how He wants you to handle things. You can also use the free downloadable sheets located at DOMELifePublishing.com

NOTES

Day 146: The Same Spirit

GO DEEPER!

1. Are you using your gifts fully or are you slacking off? How do you know?
2. Have a talk with God today about the gifts that you have received.
3. Write your reflection about your talk, on a sheet of paper, with today's date, and place it in your "For God" container. You can also use the free downloadable sheets located at DOMELifePublishing.com

NOTES

Day 147: Jesus Is Our Grapevine

GO DEEPER!

Do you recall the game called "Grapevine"? It was a game that, for most of us, was something that we first learned in elementary school. Do you remember how it was played? Most likely, your teacher had you and your classmates seated in chairs or on the floor, side-by-side. Then your teacher whispered a phrase in the ear of one student and then told the student to repeat the phrase into the ear of the student next to them. This process would continue until the last student received a whispered message. At that time, the teacher would tell the last student to repeat aloud the phrase. The phrase spoken is completely different from the initial phrase shared by the teacher. The students laugh hysterically when they hear the variations shared, student after student. Finally, the teacher would share the correct phrase and then explain the lesson behind the activity.

1. If Jesus is our grapevine, and we are attached to him, in what ways can you share his lessons and parables? How can you share the stories of his healings?
2. Like the Grapevine game, the words shared in the Bible are not always exactly as spoken. It is a collection of reflections, written by men, who journaled their experiences and those of other people. There are of course poems, songs, and letters that we assume were not edited by scribes ordered by leaders to transcribe for publication. The Bible has accounts of prophecies spoken by prophets that were then written by themselves or their companion scribes to be read to the masses.
3. The accounts of Jesus were written decades after his ascension, some from first account witnesses and others who went around like journalists interviewing the people, and taking the information and writing about it. There weren't any recording devices during that era. So there is no document or book that we can guarantee has a perfect accounting of conversations and events. Taking this into consideration, today's activity will allow you to share freely the sentiments as credited to Jesus. This isn't an exercise of regurgitating quotes. It's about expressing the loving Light that he possessed.
4. In what ways can you be like the child in the Grapevine game today?
5. At the end of the day, take notes about how this experience makes you feel.

NOTES

Day 148: God Is All in All

GO DEEPER!

1. Search your Bible or Concordance for the verses that mention God as Alpha and Omega. You already have one here, from today's message. What comes to your mind when you read these scriptures?
2. What does it mean to you when God is quoted as saying, that He is the Alpha and Omega (first and last)?
3. What does this representation mean in your life?

NOTES

Day 149: Temptation in Marriage

GO DEEPER!

How you conduct yourself says everything about how you are. It tells everyone the type of person you are, versus the one you want the world to believe.

1. What kind of person are you?
2. If you identify as a Christian, what type of Christian are you?
3. If you're married, what kind of husband/wife are you?
4. What does your life say about you? How is it aligned or contradictory to how you live?
5. In your opinion, what does it mean to be faithful?
6. What does God mean when He calls on us to be faithful?
7. Do you see yourself as the bride of Christ?
   [Please refer to Day 1 in Seek Him, Volume 1]
8. How are you being tempted to stray from your marriage to God and Jesus?
9. In what ways does your human marriage align with or contradict your spiritual marriage with God and Jesus?
10. If you're not married to another human, how would you like your marriage to be aligned to God and Jesus?

NOTES

Day 150: Getting in God's Way

GO DEEPER!

1. What are you interfering with that you should release over to God?
2. How has your interference hindered the situation?
3. Why do you keep interfering?
4. How can you begin releasing your grip of interference?
5. Add your answers to your "For God" container. Write today's date. Release them to Him. You can also use the free downloadable sheets located at DOMELifePublishing.com

NOTES

Day 151: Obedience

GO DEEPER!

1. Imagine the blessings that you have ignored and did not receive because they weren't packaged or presented in a way that you expected.
2. Are you blocking your blessings because of the blockers that you have put in place?
3. How will you address these blockers so that you can pray to God to remove them?

NOTES

Day 152: Membership, Ministry, and Mission

GO DEEPER!

1. How will you put God first today?
2. How will you best use your gifts today?
3. At the end of the day, or even tomorrow, consider journaling a reflection of how you put God first and used your gifts.

NOTES

Day 153: What Have You Done For Me Lately?

GO DEEPER!

1. What will you do today, to live life on and with purpose?
2. Who will you spend precious moments with today?

NOTES

Day 154: How Do You Feel About Your Life?

GO DEEPER!

1. Describe your life.
2. How do you feel about it?
3. What do you like about it?
4. What do you dislike about it?
5. If you don't like it then why don't you do something to change it?
6. What troubles you about your life?
7. What have you done to change your life for the better?
8. What have you avoided doing because you are afraid?
9. What thrills and excites you about your life?
10. If today was your last day in this life, what would you do? Where would you go? Who would you spend time with?

Today, do one or more of the things you listed in step 10 above. Attempt making a positive change to one of the things you're afraid of, that you listed in step 8.

NOTES

MONTH SIX: CHALLENGING THE STATUS QUO

Day 155: Grace

GO DEEPER!

God favored you, in spite of your enemies. Our blessings keep coming in. As we free ourselves from guilt and shame we realize that God has ALREADY forgiven us for our sins. Then we will see the many blessings flowing in. If we spend our time punishing ourselves, we overlook the gifts that God has for us. If you can't see the gifts and blessings, then you need to look around and within. See the ways that God's grace and mercy have blessed you.

1. Think of at least one blessing that you received today. What makes it a blessing?
2. What is so special about this thing? How does it make you feel?
3. What will you do today to celebrate this blessing? How will you share your blessing with others?
4. God shows you grace every day. How will you pay it forward to others?
5. Why do you think that you struggle with blessing others with grace?
6. Imagine if God stopped blessing you with grace, how would you feel? How would your life be different than it is today?

NOTES

Day 156: Jesus As Our Wayshower

GO DEEPER!

1. Turn to any book in the New Testament.
2. Look for passages that highlight the writer's recollection of Jesus, what he said and did.
3. Read and reflect on those passages. Visualize Jesus saying and doing these things in front of you. Visualize yourself as a follower. Spending time with him outdoors and in the temples. Listening to him, watching him do the impossible, and feeling his presence.
4. How does it make you feel?
5. What did it inspire you to do and say today?
6. How did it alter your thinking throughout the day?

NOTES

Day 157: Temptation Costs More Than You Can Afford

GO DEEPER!

1. What are your weak points, that expose you and leave you vulnerable to temptation?
2. What can you do to strengthen those weak points so that you are less exposed and vulnerable?
3. Who do you interact with that you know is a distraction, bad influence, or tempter/temptress?
4. What can you do to remove these individuals from your life, or limit their influence on it?

Throughout your day today, be mindful of the lures to take your mind off of what you're supposed to be doing. Note the intensity and frequency of these lures. Note how you felt during and after you noticed that you were being tempted to stray from your course.

NOTES

Day 158: It Isn't About You

GO DEEPER!

1. Write down the ways that God has blessed you so far this year.
2. Have a conversation with God today, and express your gratitude for these blessings.

Each day share your blessings with others. Even if it's only one person. Share. Each day be a blessing to others. Pay forward what God has given you.

NOTES

Day 159: Thank God in Advance

GO DEEPER!

Make a conscious effort to thank God throughout your day. For not just the big things but also for the little things. Thank Him when you find the matching sock that disappeared from the laundry. Thank Him for starting your car. Thank Him for getting you to work or school on time and without incident. Thank Him for holding your tongue so you didn't speak the words that you were thinking about someone. Thank Him for reminding you of something you had forgotten to do or someone you had forgotten to contact. Thank Him every time someone is nice, especially when it wasn't expected. Thank Him when a stranger says "Hello" or "Good morning". Thank Him when your pet doesn't destroy something that you value.

NOTES

Day 160: Live in Your Situation

GO DEEPER!

1. What things do you desire that you may be growing anxious over?
2. Have a conversation with God today. Speak to Him about the things that you want and need. Write down the things that you can recall from that conversation.
3. What are some of the takeaways from your conversation?
4. Did having that talk bring you peace, calm, comfort, or just more anxiety and fear?
5. In what ways?

NOTES

Day 161: Power in Words

GO DEEPER!

Try Something: Every time you notice that you're thinking and saying something negative, try to catch yourself. If you recall, we practiced this on Day 42 in Seek Him, Volume 1, and on Day 75 in Seek Him Workbook 1. Quickly repeat a word or phrase that helps to disrupt you, such as, "Erase, erase, erase" or "Cancel, cancel, cancel" or "The devil is a liar". Or anything that can cause you to stop thinking or saying whatever it is that you know is not a loving reflection of God. Words have power. Be mindful of the power that you wield.

Take note of how you felt each time you caught yourself mid-thought or mid-sentence. Just like all habits, it comes with practice. Refraining from negative speech will take time. Some days you will thrive and other days it will feel like you can't stop messing up. It's okay. God knows your heart. Don't stop trying. Don't give up.

NOTES

Day 162: God's Wisdom

GO DEEPER!

God provides you with gifts that you build skills upon. The more information that you retain, the more knowledge that you gain. The more lessons that you learn, the more wisdom that becomes yours to use or waste. But it is only possible because of God.

How will you best use your gifts and wisdom to glorify Him?

NOTES

Day 163: What Will It Take?

GO DEEPER!

Answer the questions below. Write down the first things that come to mind. Don't overthink it.

Session 1

1. What will it take for you to believe and trust that God is your best answer?
2. What will it take for you to freely release your problems, issues, and concerns to Him?
3. What are your fears? What's holding you back?
4. Now, put this book down and walk away for an hour or more.

Session 2

After some time has passed, return and answer the questions again. Don't look at your previous answers.

1. What will it take for you to believe and trust that God is your best answer?
2. What will it take for you to freely release your problems, issues, and concerns to Him?
3. What are your fears? What's holding you back?

Note any differences between Session 1 and Session 2. Reflect upon those differences.

Think about the questions and your answers, and then do something to release yourself into God's capable hands.

NOTES

Day 164: Our Tests

GO DEEPER!

Reflecting upon what we already discussed in today's message, let's dig deeper. Starting first with the menfolk...

An attractive, intelligent woman can distract a man to the point that he can make a complete fool of himself. She can manipulate him into paying less attention to his own girlfriend/wife. She can make him look at what appears to be her values and virtues, and marvel over them. She becomes the thing he idols, worships even. Then he will pick at and tear down everything he believes to be flaws in his wife/girlfriend. It always starts innocently. That's how the enemy gets you. It's a mirage. Smoke and mirrors. The 10 to 20 percent of qualities this woman seemingly brings to the table always negates the 80 to 90 percent your wife/girlfriend has to offer. But a man who has been hooked and reeled in like a barracuda will always think this other woman has 80 to 90 percent of what he wants. The enemy convinces him that somehow his wife/girlfriend is the one lacking. Her 80 to 90 percent now looks like a mere 10 to 20 percent. Only with and through God can the truth be revealed. Only God can show you that you have been, as the saying goes, "hoodwinked...bamboozled...led astray...." The enemy is here to confuse you and convince you to cause chaos in your life. He is the father of lies, tricking you into believing that his darkness is actually light.

Men, when your focus is on God, your discernment helps you to identify what is from God versus what is a trap of the enemy. You learn to identify the subtle and overt flirting. You're mindful of the body language, frequent body contact, and other baits used. You will avoid them like the plague. You will never invite them to have a part in your life that should be reserved to only those closest and dearest to you. You will never allow yourself to be alone with them. You won't have to learn the hard way to never ever let them into your home, hotel room, or private office. They will never have private access to you. Men must learn to stop trying to save everyone—especially women! If they need counseling let them find a counselor in church, online, or through their job. If they ask you, encourage them to turn to these valuable resources. Tell them to pray first for the answer. The "liar" will rebuke the thought of that, which then reveals itself to you, and proves true intent. When you believe that you're called to save this woman, you have fallen into the trap. You are not a savior. Stay in your lane. Know your role.

The same is true of God's daughters. Whether it be males or females attempting to trap you as prey, with your focus on God you will always see them coming. You can easily adjust your thinking so that their attempts to steer you off your path always result in a big FAIL! Women, we must be watchful of the woman who eagerly wants to befriend us. The one always smiling in your face, but her eyes show anything but pure thoughts about you. Pray to our Father that He opens your eyes and shows you this woman's true essence and intent. And how best to deal with her—and keep a safe distance. Women, watch the advances of men. Like the lion they can be crafty as they wait until you are alone to pounce and attack.

1. How are you being tested by God?
2. What do you think that He wants you to learn from this experience?
3. Who (or what) is the enemy using to tempt you, and how?
4. Why do you think that you're able to be tempted?
5. What will you do to refocus on your path and purpose, so that you can pass the tests and not be overcome by the temptations?

NOTES

Day 165: It May Not Be As Soon As You Want

GO DEEPER!

1. In practicing patience, what things are you still waiting for (even if impatiently)?
2. Write them down on a sheet of paper, with today's date, and place them in your "For God" container. You can also use the free downloadable sheets located at DOMELifePublishing.com

NOTES

Day 166: Fight the "Liar"

GO DEEPER!

1. What attacks are you facing today?
2. If applicable, when do you think that the attacks become more or less severe (in frequency or intensity?
3. How do you feel about these attacks and how you're being attacked?
4. Do you write in a journal about these attacks?
5. Does writing help you or cause you to feel more anxious? In what ways?
6. What support do you have from family, friends, and associates?
7. What support do you have from mental health professionals or a coach?
8. What support do you have from your minister, pastor, or other religious leaders?
9. How often do you speak with God about these attacks?
10. How do your conversations with God leave you feeling afterward?
11. If you have not spoken to anyone about these attacks and how you're feeling, why?

Spend some time with God today, and speak to Him about how you're feeling. Ask Him for guidance. Ask Him to provide you what you need to persevere and overcome. Ask Him to connect you with the right people who can serve as positive support systems.

NOTES

Day 167: Pray, Study, and Meditate Daily

GO DEEPER!

1. Open your Bible or Bible app, to wherever you want. If you're opening the physical book, you can just grab the pages and flip them open. If you're using a Bible app, you can just select the first book that your eyes see.
2. Spend at least 30 minutes today reading the passages.
3. Take notes. Write down which book(s) and chapter(s) that you read.
4. What are your thoughts about these passages? How did it make you feel reading them?
5. What impressions were you left with? Did you feel empowered, challenged, inspired, or something else?
6. If you are using a Bible app or have access to the Internet, compare the translation(s) you are reading to the Orthodox Jewish Bible (OJB) translation, so you can see both Hebrew and English words— since the Bible was originally written in Hebrew and Aramaic, then translated to Greek, and then Latin (and other languages), then Olde English, and modern English. Search online for translations of all Hebrew words that are not already translated in the OJB.
7. How did it feel to include Hebrew in your study?
8. Was there a slight or significant difference in the English translation in comparison to the Hebrew text? In what ways?
9. Can you see how the Hebrew words and phrases could have been mistranslated by the Greeks and English?

As we progress we will explore this more, as history, culture, customs, and other considerations must be factored into our reading and studying of the Bible. You could be wrongly reading and applying information because you don't know what the people meant in ancient times.

NOTES

Day 168: No Limits

GO DEEPER!
1. What big, bold moves do you plan to pursue today?
2. What big, bold decisions will you make today?
3. What big, bold thoughts will you entertain today?

NOTES

Day 169: Good for You

GO DEEPER!

Try Something: If you aren't physically active each week, working out outdoors, in a gym, or at home—take 35 minutes today to do the following:

1. Walk briskly for 5 minutes to warm up, then stop and stretch for 5 minutes. Be mindful of your breathing—your inhale and exhale. As you stretch, pay attention to each area and notice any tension. Hold the stretch for 20 seconds before moving on to the next body part. This is the time to tell your body what you want and need it to do. In a way, you're communicating to your body the importance of working in partnership with you, while you're preparing your mind to push past fear and doubt. Does that make sense? Hopefully so.
2. After your 5 minutes are up resume your walk for 20 minutes.
3. At the end of your walk, stretch for another 5 minutes. Did any tense areas become relaxed? Do you feel stronger and more alert than you did at the beginning of your workout?

Hopefully, you broke a sweat. Hopefully, you felt good, feel good, and feel recharged. Try to make this your habit at least 3 times per week. It's good for your mind, heart, body, spirit, and soul.

NOTES

Day 170: Speak For Others

GO DEEPER!

1. Pray for one or more people today. Be specific, intentional, be focused, and be sincere.
2. Who are they?
3. Why do you want to pray for them?
4. What are they going through that you want to speak to God about?

Make sure that you are free of distractions and that you set aside the time to speak to God on these individuals' behalf. He already knows their situation. He's already determined the outcome. That's not the point. This is an exercise about your willingness to speak to Him about someone other than yourself.

NOTES

Day 171: Imagine Your Life

GO DEEPER!

Write down your prayer for today and place it in your "For God" container. Write today's date. Release it to Him! You can also use the free downloadable sheets located at DOMELifePublishing.com

NOTES

Day 172: Clarity

GO DEEPER!

1. What obstacle is before you that seems too big to overcome?
2. Why do you think that you can't get past, break through, tear down, climb over, or dig under this obstacle?
3. Why are you reluctant to hand this obstacle over to God?
4. Have you convinced yourself that you have turned it over to God but that things are just moving too slow?
    Think about what this belief says about you and how you see God.
5. Is it possible that you simply don't see the big picture and all of the details?
6. Is it possible that your eyes aren't "opened" enough to see?

NOTES

Day 173: You May Know Him, But Do You Glorify Him?

GO DEEPER!

What would you like to add to your "For God" container today? Add it. Write today's date. Then try to let it go. Holding on to it is you micromanaging God. Trust Him to handle it.

NOTES

Day 174: Truth, Always Be Revealed

GO DEEPER!

1. What lie are you keeping from someone?
2. How long have you been keeping this lie a secret?
3. Why do you think that keeping this lie a secret is worth it?
4. Is there something happening in your life right now that you are struggling with telling the truth about? Are you contemplating not telling the truth? Why?
5. What are the risks and rewards of telling the truth?
6. What are the risks and perceived rewards of telling the lie?
7. How does it make you feel to tell and keep lies?
8. Do you convince yourself that certain lies are "small" lies, and thus, are acceptable?
9. So how does telling "big" lies make you feel?
10. How do you feel when someone lies to you? Why?
11. If you don't like being lied to, then are you not a hypocrite? How does that make you feel?

Ponder these questions and your answers. Reflect upon them throughout the day.

NOTES

Day 175: May Your Pain Still Be Your Blessing

GO DEEPER!

Release your pain and discomfort into your "For God" container. Write exactly how you feel, what you're going through, what you're fearing, what confuses you, what is causing you pain and discomfort. Release it all to God. Write today's date. Then fold up the paper and put it in the container. You can also use the free downloadable sheets located at DOMELifePublishing.com

NOTES

Day 176: Rejoice in His Work

GO DEEPER!

You can be employed, unemployed, self-employed, under-employed—it doesn't matter because our most important job is serving God and helping His children. Let's get to work!!!!

What will you do today?

Ask God, "*Father what do You want me to do today? What do You want me to focus my attention on today? Who do you want me to serve today?*"

Write in the notes section below your reflection from that conversation.

NOTES

Day 177: God Is the Solution

GO DEEPER!

1. What are your go-to verses in the Bible that you read or recite to help bring you calm, clarity, peace, or reassurance?
2. Read aloud or recite from memory at least one of the verses, slowly, allowing yourself the chance to fully take in the words, message, meaning, and feelings that arise. Don't rush this. It's not a race. There's a reason that you're drawn to read or recite this verse, allow yourself the time to ingest the nourishment that comes from speaking these words. Feed your mind, spirit, and soul.
3. After you finish, just sit as still and comfortably as you can, in quiet, and just be present with God. Don't put thought into it. Don't set a timer. Just be. He will guide you. Trust in Him.

NOTES

Day 178: Endurance

GO DEEPER!

Try Something: Today, focus on not complaining about your life—but instead, praising God for the opportunities, lessons, and blessings.

1. Who in your life do you know that has amazing spiritual endurance?
2. Speak to them today and see if they are willing to help you, mentor you, coach you on how to build your own spiritual endurance.

NOTES

Day 179: Steer Me Clear

GO DEEPER!

Reflecting on today's message in Seek Him, Volume 2, write down your "Not here, not now, not ever". Make sure that it is not just your declaration about others, but also about you—and then place the list (with today's date on it) into your "For God" container. You can also use the free downloadable sheets located at DOMELifePublishing.com

NOTES

Day 180: Impatience

GO DEEPER!

Try Something: Throughout the day, take note of the times when your impatience becomes obvious to you and/or to others.

1. What triggered your impatience?
2. What happened when you became impatient?
3. How did you feel?
4. Now think about your impatience towards the goals that you are pursuing. Be honest with yourself. What is preventing you from completing your tasks and goals?

Reflect upon all of this when you consider your impatience and interference with God.

NOTES

Day 181: In God's Sight

GO DEEPER!

If possible, recite in the mirror, your "SPEAK YOUR TRUTH" affirmations from today. Look at yourself. Keep repeating your affirmations until they become your truth—until you feel confident and empowered to take on the day like the King/Queen that God made you to be.

NOTES

Day 182: Is This Global Karma?

GO DEEPER!

1. What are your thoughts about today's Reflection?
2. What do you think about global karma?
3. Do you think that what we put into the world is returned to us?
4. What will your focus be on today?

NOTES

Day 183: Let Hate Motivate You to Love

GO DEEPER!

1. Who do you want to pray for today? Why?
2. How do you think that God's intervention (and the answer to your prayer) would benefit them?
3. Pray this forward to your "For God" container. Yep, write it down, with today's date, and place it in the container to release the issue to God. You can also use the free downloadable sheets located at DOMELifePublishing.com

NOTES

Day 184: Goodness From Within

GO DEEPER!
1. What thing or things would you like to atone for and make right?
2. What steps must you take to make right your wrong?
3. If there is no conceivable way to right your wrong, for whatever reason, what steps can you take to atone to God and begin healing yourself from within so that you can mend the self-inflicted wound?

NOTES

MONTH SEVEN: CHALLENGING THE DISCOMFORT

Day 185: Rethink Christmas

GO DEEPER!

1. If you celebrate Christmas, why do you do it?
2. What are your plans for Christmas this year?
3. How will you spend that day and week?
4. What are your plans for gift giving? Why?
5. What kind of traditions do you take part in during Christmas?
6. What kind of traditions would you like to start? Why?

NOTES

Day 186: Don't Test God

GO DEEPER!

1. Can you tell the difference between God's voice and the enemy's?
2. How can you tell the difference?
3. Can you tell the difference between God's voice and your ego? How?
4. How do you identify the enemy's tempting lures throughout the day?
5. How do you handle the temptation, both small and large?
6. How has your ego gotten in the way of your internal peace? How has your ego caused drama?
7. How can you control your ego?
8. In what ways can you condition yourself to place God's voice as a priority over yours and anyone else?

NOTES

Day 187: Absolution

GO DEEPER!

Try Something: Below, write down a prayer to God. What do you want to release to Him? What do you want to be freed from? What do you need help with? Share this in a prayer. Feel free to include this prayer in your "For God" container. You can also use the free downloadable sheets located at DOMELifePublishing.com

NOTES

Day 188: Righteous Like Noah

GO DEEPER!

1. Reflecting over the story of Noah, in what ways are you like Noah?
2. In what ways would you like to be more like Noah?
3. What do you admire most about Noah?

NOTES

Day 189: Why Not?

GO DEEPER!

1. What are you not pursuing because you keep making excuses?
2. What were you denied because someone said you couldn't do it or couldn't have it?
3. What opportunities are you ready to say "Why Not" to?

NOTES

Day 190: He Heals

GO DEEPER!

1. What would you like to be healed from?
2. In David's song, he praised God for healing him from things that tormented him. What has God healed you from, recently, or in the past, that you would like to thank Him for?
3. Who would you like to pray for that needs healing?
4. Recite the prayer from today's message in Seek Him, Volume 2. As you say the prayer, personalize it, and allow yourself to speak freely; let the words flow from you.
5. After saying the prayer write on a piece of paper the things and issues that you are praying for God to heal. Write down your praise and thanksgiving for all that God has healed you from recently, or in the past. Then write today's date and put it in your "For God" container, to release it to Him. You can also use the free downloadable sheets located at DOMELifePublishing.com

NOTES

Day 191: Will You Be The Redeemed?

GO DEEPER!

1. If you believe in the 144,000 that John wrote of in the Book of Revelation, reflect on how you would feel if you weren't the chosen, but instead one of the many left behind?
2. If you don't believe in the 144,000, what if you're wrong about what you are thinking and believing?
3. Do you think there is anything that you can do to be redeemed and be chosen? Why?
4. Even if there isn't an actual 144,000 or there is but the number is much greater, why wouldn't you still live your life each day as Jesus did (and taught), with the hope of being selected?

In the GREATER CONTEXT chapter of this workbook, you can find an explanation and analysis of the 144,000, so you can further form your thinking and opinion.

NOTES

Day 192: Worthy of His Calling

GO DEEPER!

Below please find a partial list of people from the Bible that were called by God.

Noah: called to leave behind everyone and everything except for what and whom God selected, so that God could wipe out life and start over.

Abraham: God called on him to be faithful and obedient, to be rewarded with a son that would start a limitless bloodline.

Moses: called on to deliver Israelites from Egypt, be a prophet and share God's laws, help formalize the hierarchy amongst the families, and prepare them for the promised land, even though he would never step foot in the promised land. God let him see it but he couldn't go.

Samson: God provided him with unspeakable strength and was told to never cut his hair—as that was supposedly the source of his strength. Of course, we know that God was the source, however, it kept him focused on being obedient.

Esther: was called by God to deliver Israel from total extermination by Haman.

Daniel: he was a regular Joe Blow, low-key guy who was obedient to God. He remained loyal to his Jewish faith, even while assimilating into Persian culture.

Jeremiah: called to be a prophet and to speak verbatim what God said to him

Isaiah: called to be a prophet and representative for all of Israel

Ezekiel: called to be a prophet while in exile

Apostle Paul: a persecutor of early disciples of Christ, on his road to Damascus to arrest the disciples and return them to Jerusalem, Jesus appeared in a bright light and blinded him for three days. Paul was called on by God to spread the teachings of Jesus.

David: was called by God to be the King of Israel, even though Samuel didn't see in David the characteristics that were typical of monarchs.

Mary: was called to birth and be the mother of Jesus, the Messiah, and understand that he would be sacrificed for mankind.

Joseph (Mary's husband): was called to marry her and be the "step-dad" to Jesus

1. Looking at this partial list, what do you have in common with one or more of these people?
2. What do their situations all have in common?

NOTES

Day 193: Don't Be Deceived

GO DEEPER!

1. If Jesus descended today, describe what he would see in your life?
2. Are you ready for his return? Why?

NOTES

Day 194: Control Your Heart

GO DEEPER!

1. In what ways has your heart been deceived because you didn't let it work in tandem with your mind?
2. List some examples of people in the Bible (that inspire you) who were aligned with God's heart.
3. Share why you think their hearts were aligned with His.

NOTES

Day 195: Spiritual Maturity

GO DEEPER!
1. In what ways have you matured spiritually over the past year?
2. How can you tell that you have matured?
3. Where would you like to improve spiritually?

NOTES

Day 196: Reconciliation to God

GO DEEPER!

Even if you're physically circumcised, most likely you aren't of Jewish descent and faith, so the procedure wasn't done as part of the covenant with God. But even if you are of Jewish lineage, have you circumcised your heart?

We are all called to circumcise our hearts—cut away and discard that which is not desired by God, to expose and reveal your heart to Him and others. Tomorrow, we will discuss this further. Today, just reflect on what that means to you and God.

NOTES

Day 197: Circumcised in Him

GO DEEPER!

Picking up where we left off yesterday, let's talk about circumcising our hearts.

1. What needs to be cut away from your heart?
2. What useless emotions, feelings, issues are you carrying around?
3. What needs to be cut away and discarded so you can spiritually and physically free?

NOTES

Day 198: Be Steadfast

GO DEEPER!

1. List at least two (2) people from the Bible that were firm and immovable in their faith and obedience to God.
2. List at least two (2) people in your family or inner circle who you would describe in the same way.
3. Which people throughout history can you think of that demonstrated that steadfastness?

NOTES

Day 199: First Adam to Last

GO DEEPER!

Let's compare the first Adam [Genesis] to the last Adam (Jesus).

Genesis Adam

- Created by God to reproduce human life with Eve [First generation]
- Called to help build God's Kingdom on Earth.
- Told that Eve was his equal and they were to align as one
- Was given the responsibility to steward the land and all of God's creations
- Was told not to "eat" from the "tree" of the knowledge of good and evil
- He chose to listen to Satan (serpent), disobeyed God, and "ate" the "fruit"; He sinned
- His disobedience caused him to be cursed and banned from the Garden
- His relationship with Eve was fractured; His relationship with God was fractured
- Working the land became labor-intensive
- He and Eve gave birth to three sons: Cain, Abel (killed by Cain), and Seth (born after Abel killed)
- Seth [second generation] father's the line that eventually led to Jesus [76th generation according to Book of Luke]

Jesus [Last Adam]

- Lived as a spirit who seemingly appears on Earth throughout the Old Testament as God's unnamed Angel
- Born to a human mother, Mary, made possible by God
- Called by God to save humankind from sin and the spiritual death that comes from sin.
- He taught people the Truth about God, God's Kingdom, a government in heaven that will bring peace to Earth
- He taught about eternal life, about our spiritual beingness, and living by example
- Jesus knew he had to fulfill all of God's Old Testament prophecies, which also included self-sacrifice (persecution and crucifixion), and then leave this world and ascend back to God's realm.
- Healed people, raised people from the dead
- Never sinned; Perfect man
- Betrayed (by Judas Iscariot) and denied by Peter

- The Sadducees and Pharisees plotted to kill him
- Was beaten, tortured, ridiculed, tormented, nailed up, and left to die

1. When you compare these two lists, what differences do you note?
2. How did Jesus rectify what Adam did?
3. Jesus said he came to separate, to create division, to destroy the world of Satan, and through teaching God's Truth, people will choose to either align with Him or with sin. Reflecting on this, what do believers need to do to help save souls?

NOTES

Day 200: Faithful Over The Household

GO DEEPER!

1. How well are you taking care of your household?
2. What kind of leader are you?
3. How well do you manage the resources gifted to you?

Take the next several minutes praying to God about your household, your role in that household, your leadership style, and your stewardship. Ask Him the questions that you would like answers to. Pray for His intervention where you need it most, whether you know it or not. Pray for the strength, courage, clarity, and discernment in the areas where He knows you need it. Don't skip this step. If you truly want to be faithful over your household, you need to speak to God every single day for His guidance. Don't be passive with something He has entrusted you with.

NOTES

Day 201: One Flesh in Marriage

GO DEEPER!

For Married People

1. If you're married, what are the strengths of and in your marriage?
2. What are the weaknesses, weak points, areas that can be easily penetrated under attack?
3. What areas of your marriage have been attacked? In what ways?

For Divorced People

1. What are some of the reasons your marriage failed?
2. What weaknesses did you not identify early enough, that made it easier for the enemy to attack your marriage?

For Widows/Widowers

1. What were the strengths of your marriage?
2. What were the weaknesses in your marriage that you learned from?

For Single, Never Married People

1. If you're thinking about getting married: What do you think God expects of you if you choose to get married one day?
2. What are the weaknesses that you need to strengthen or be secured within God?
3. So that the two of you are working together in partnership, as one flesh, what strengths does a potential spouse need to have to help compensate for your weaknesses, and/or further complement your strengths?

NOTES

Day 202: Women Builders

GO DEEPER!

1. Building upon today's message in Seek Him, Volume 2, in what ways are you encouraging, supporting, and advocating for women and girls in the following environments and scenarios:

- Within the church (in ministry)
- In schools
- In the arts (in schools and other areas)
- In STREAM (science, technology, robotics, engineering, agriculture, math) education
- In the workplace
- In the military
- In government
- On social media sites

2. God said that man and woman were to be equal and rule the animals and land together, not over each other. In what ways are you doing your part to protect and advocate for God's daughters who are constantly being reduced to tiers below man and sometimes being treated equally to or below animals?

3. Either one of two things will happen first, you will take your last breath or Jesus will return for the days of Judgment. Whichever comes first, what will God say about your advocacy for women and girls?

4. If you took your last breath today, would you be satisfied with what you have done to support, encourage, and advocate for women and girls?

NOTES

Day 203: A Confident Heart

GO DEEPER!

This activity may take a little time, or not, depending on how honest you're willing to be with yourself.
1. Write down everything that you're stressing over
2. Which of these things is God incapable of fixing, handling, solving, saving?
3. Reflect on this. Let it really sink it.
4. Why are you still stressing and holding on?
5. When will you make up your mind to let go and let God do what only He can do?

NOTES

Day 204: Selfless Service

GO DEEPER!

1. What is your mission?
2. What have you been called to do?
3. What does your heart feel pulled to do in your community, state, or in the world?
4. If you're not sure, then it's time to pray and seek guidance and clarity from God.

Spend the next 15 minutes to an hour, or as long as needed, for you to have an uninterrupted conversation with God, to begin seeing and hearing what He wants for you.

NOTES

Day 205: Seeing God Everywhere

GO DEEPER!

1. Can you see God in others?
2. In what ways?
3. Reflect upon a time when you failed to see God in a situation.
4. Reflect upon a time when you thought God was involved in a situation, had "His Hand" in something, that you later found out wasn't the case.
5. What has that taught you about discernment?

NOTES

Day 206: What Will You Do For Your Friend?

GO DEEPER!

1. What type of friend are you?
2. Are you a cheerful giver to your friends?
3. Can your friends depend on you to keep promises and protect their hearts?
4. Can your friends count on you to be there in the good times and bad times?
5. Be completely honest, are you the type of friend who is excited about your friends' successes and achievements, doing everything you can to support them? Or do you downplay, hate on, or "rain on their parade", out of envy?
6. How often do you pray for your friends?
7. If you don't pray for them, or rarely do, consider why?
8. Pray to God for your friendships and to help you be a better friend.

NOTES

Day 207: Never Ever Give Up

GO DEEPER!

1. List three (3) goals that you are pursuing that have taken longer than you had hoped, that you have contemplated walking away from.
2. List three (3) dreams that you believe God has given you that you sometimes think aren't still made for you, or feel are too far out of your reach.
3. If God has given you a vision, dream, promise, and He keeps reminding you of this vision, dream, promise—then obviously what He has planned for you is for you—so do you doubt Him?
4. Ask God to provide you with insight on the vision, dream, promise, and write down your frustrations, fears, and desires on a piece of paper, with today's date, and put it in your "For God" container. You can also use the free downloadable sheets located at DOMELifePublishing.com

NOTES

Day 208: Fools Make More Fools

GO DEEPER!

1. In an argument, are you more inclined to argue, remain silent, try to de-escalate it, or walk away?
2. Why?
3. Describe how you speak and behave in an argument.
4. Why do you think that people choose to argue?
5. At what point has an argument gotten out of control, and entered the danger zone?
6. What do you think would be different in your life if you chose to do one of the other options listed above? For instance, if you normally argue, how would things be different in your life if you chose instead to remain silent, de-escalate things, or walk away from an argument?
7. What would you prefer to do when you find yourself in a disagreement?
8. Can you visualize Jesus going round after round in an argument or having a screaming match with someone? What examples does the Bible share of how Jesus handled disagreements?

NOTES

Day 209: Mouth Full Of What?

GO DEEPER!

Be honest with yourself...

1. Are you an optimist or a pessimist?
2. Do you focus more on the positive or negative in scenarios?
3. Do you tend to speak positively or negatively?
4. When people speak about you do they call you a negative or positive person? Do they joke about you being a drama queen/king?
5. Write down your visualization of how Jesus spoke to everyday people.
6. We say that Jesus spoke with love, but what does that mean to you?

NOTES

Day 210: Setting the Example For Your Household

GO DEEPER!

Abraham and Sarah set an example for their household; Isaac and Rebekah set an example for their household; Jacob and Rachel set an example for their household. All three couples set good, not-so-good, and poor examples.

1. What examples did each couple set?
2. What examples did each husband set?
3. What examples did each wife set?
4. What example are you setting for your household?

NOTES

Day 211: Your Obligation

GO DEEPER!

1. What do you feel obliged to do for God's Kingdom?

NOTES

Day 212: Supporting God Is Faith

GO DEEPER!

On Day 59, in Seek Him, Volume 1, we dug briefly into the topic of faith. Do you recall? If not, be sure to re-read the message. Review your notes. What parts or sections of the message resonated with you? Take a few minutes to reflect on that message and today's message.

NOTES

Day 213: Death Is No Master

GO DEEPER!

1. What does death mean to you?
2. Do you fear it? Why?
3. If you fear death, is it spiritual or physical death? Or both?
4. Speak to God about your fears. Write them down, include today's date on the paper, and put it in your "For God" container. You can also use the free downloadable sheets located at DOMELifePublishing.com

NOTES

Day 214: Feed My Sheep

GO DEEPER!

Jesus asked Simon Peter if he loved him and then he told him to "feed my sheep".

How are you feeding his sheep?

NOTES

MONTH EIGHT: CHALLENGING THE LIES

Day 215: Your Lying Words

GO DEEPER!

This exercise may take some time to complete, so make sure that you have set aside at least 20 to 30 minutes to complete it.

1. Describe your church. What does a first-time visitor see, hear, and experience?
2. Describe a typical service at your church?
3. How does your church manage offerings, tithes, and other collections?
4. What are the demographics of your congregation?
5. What are the demographics of your church leaders?
6. What are the tenets and mission statement of your church?
7. What does it take to become a member of your church?
8. Describe your congregation's outreach to your local community [within four square miles of the church].
9. List some of the ministries your church focuses on.
10. How are the leaders in your church compensated for their service, if applicable?
11. In what ways does your church meet or fail to meet the image it portrays online on its website (if applicable)?
12. How are congregants taught the Bible and trained to serve?

We will be examining this and other things tomorrow and again in a few days. For now, just reflect on what you have written today.

NOTES

Day 216: Hijacking The Church

GO DEEPER!

In the Book of Revelation, Jesus told John to observe and then provide his assessment of the seven early churches. Below is what was written.

1. **Ephesus**: was known for their hard work and not giving up, they separated themselves from the wicked; however, they were admonished for having forsaken their first love [Revelation 2:1-7]
2. **Smyrna**: admired for enduring tribulation and poverty; they were told they would suffer persecution [Revelation 2:8-11]
3. **Pergamum**: was described as located where Satan's seat is; needs to repent for allowing false teachers to teach the congregation [Revelation 2:12-17]
4. **Thyatira**: known for their charity, whose latter works far-surpassed their former works, however, they tolerated the teachings of a false prophetess [Revelation 2:18-29]
5. **Sardis**: although they had a good reputation, they were admonished for being dead; they were told they needed to fortify themselves, repent, and return to God [Revelation 3:1-6]
6. **Philadelphia**: known for their steadfastness in faith, enduring patiently, and keeping God's word [Revelation 3:7-13]
7. **Laodicea**: was called lukewarm and insipid (lacking vigor or interest) [Revelation 3:14-22]

If Jesus was to provide a report on your church, which of the seven churches does your church best reflect? In what ways?

NOTES

Day 217: Charged With a Calling

GO DEEPER!

Read the corresponding text in Numbers 6:22-27 to get a better understanding of what is meant when they say that someone "blessed" someone during these Biblical periods. It's an Aaronic benediction that is both bold and beautiful. Also, in Romans 1:7, John's letter (in this section) is a reference to the Numbers 6 text.

It is amazing how they would tie in Old Testament sayings, promises, events, and scenarios to layer in, reinforce, bring clarity to their current situations. That proves that they were students of the Word for they were quick to reference other writers, prophets, and servants of God. Jesus was brilliant at weaving the Old Covenant in with their current experiences, to help the people see why God was rolling out a New Covenant. We must learn how to study and apply the ways, words, and prophecies of the old into our new, so that we can make sense of this world we live in, our roles in it, and what we must do to glorify God, and heal His heart.

1. What if the disciples and apostles had decided to not share their stories and Jesus' teachings, what would we have, know, and do today?

2. How would your life be today if you didn't have a relationship with Jesus?

NOTES

Day 218: The Marys'

GO DEEPER!

1. Write down your thoughts and feelings about Mary, mother of Jesus, and Mary Magdalene?
2. What are some of the things that you admire about them?
3. In what ways would you like to be more like Mary, Jesus' mother?
4. In what ways would you like to be more like Mary Magdalene?

NOTES

Day 219: Bribed to Keep a Lie

GO DEEPER!

1. Write about a time when you agreed to tell a lie because someone bribed, enticed, threatened, or scared you.
2. How did it make you feel knowing you were lying?
3. What happened? Was the truth eventually revealed?
4. What would have happened if you had told the truth or just walked away, and refused to take part in the situation?

NOTES

Day 220: Backstabbers

GO DEEPER!

1. Have you ever been betrayed?
2. How did it feel?
3. Were you ever able to trust the person again? Why?
4. Have you ever betrayed someone? Why?
5. Did you repent and rectify the situation?
6. Spend the next several minutes, or as long as you need, to pray for your relationships.

NOTES

Day 221: Death Didn't Stop Him

GO DEEPER!

1. Are you ready for your old self to die?
2. In what ways?
3. What are you ready to let go of right now?
4. What are you ready to leave behind?
5. Who are you ready to let go?
6. What habits are you ready to change for the better?
7. What habits are you ready to form to be more disciplined?

NOTES

Day 222: Time to Clean House

GO DEEPER!

1. In what ways does your church reflect the congregation that Jesus envisioned and spoke of?
2. In what ways can your church improve?

NOTES

Day 223: Jesus' RoadShow

GO DEEPER!

If you knew you would die in less than five years, what would you do starting today?

NOTES

Day 224: Choose Life

GO DEEPER!

We know that sin leads to death; it keeps us disconnected from God and out of salvation's reach. Examine your life, your household— what is at risk of being manipulated by the enemy? The enemy is the author of confusion, the prince of lies, the chief deceiver. He also projects forward what some may be tricked into believing is light— but it's not God's Light. Take an inventory of what you need to pray over and do your part to protect.

NOTES

Day 225: Rooted In God's Love

GO DEEPER!

Time to look within yourself. It's self-love check-up time.

1. What affirmations are you speaking into and over yourself?
2. What loving words are you using to describe your looks, intelligence, personality, and life?
3. Repeat today's "Speak Your Truth" aloud, looking in the mirror if possible. Repeat it until you feel it and you feel that positive energy flowing through you. If something you had written was negative, change it to something positive. Root yourself in God's love.

NOTES

Day 226: Sabbath Hypocrite

GO DEEPER!

Write a prayer to God on a sheet of paper, put today's date on it, and release it to your "For God" container. You can also use the free downloadable sheets located at DOMELifePublishing.com

NOTES

Day 227: You Are the Light

GO DEEPER!

Reflecting upon today's message in Seek Him, Volume 2, go out today sharing God's Light. You carry it with you, pour it into others. Don't hoard it. Share it. Stop delaying.

Close this book right now!

NOTES

Day 228: Without Hesitation

GO DEEPER!

1. Do you have belief, faith, and conviction like Aeneas? Or would you look at Peter and tell him about your medical condition and why you can't get up?
2. What do you think that God is expecting you to do that requires immediate action, without doubt, or hesitation?

NOTES

Day 229: Apart From God

GO DEEPER!

1. Imagine a life without God. Describe it.
2. Can you imagine loving God as deeply, fully, and unconditionally as David loved Him?
3. Imagine loving God as much as He loves you. Can you fathom that? What comes to mind when you think of this?
4. Describe how the thoughts make you feel.

NOTES

Day 230: Value in Your Giving

GO DEEPER!

Look through the Bible and find the stories of various almanot (plural of almanah): Tamar (Genesis 38); the widow that Elijah visits (1 Kings 17); and others. We know that Abigail (1 Samuel 25), Naomi, Ruth, and Orpah were widows (Ruth 1-4) however, they were not referenced as almanot, which insinuates that they still had financial means of support. Bath-Sheba (2 Samuel 11) was also a widow, but that's because King David had her husband killed and then took her as a wife, so she was financially cared for.

But what if they didn't have the support from family or new husbands? They would be regarded as an almanah. We have examples of women from the past and present, who humbly served and gave of themselves to Christ—their gifts and service far exceeding the elitists and wealthy. Even in loss, they were wealthier and more blessed than their so-called counterparts. Even when others mistreated them, ridiculed them, called them names, and tried to embarrass them, these women kept their heads up and walked with grace. We all have a lot to learn from them.

1. What have you learned from these women?

NOTES

Day 231: Truth Needs No Force

GO DEEPER!

In today's Seek Him, Volume 2 message you read about Jesus and the Samaritan woman. How does the modern Christian approach to sharing the greatness and love of God and Jesus with other people similar to or different from how Jesus engaged and embraced the Samaritan woman? In what ways are we still bound to the old way of worshipping God at designated places and times?

NOTES

Day 232: Only Believe

GO DEEPER!

Let's pick up where we left off today in SEEK HIM, Volume 2. Consider those around you. Those worrywarts, doubters, sapsuckers, and energy drainers. Let me share some examples with you. You sneeze or cough one time and they have diagnosed you with the flu. You fall behind on your bills and they tell you to rush to a bankruptcy firm to file. You argue with your spouse, and they suggest you consider separation or divorce. Your child begins testing you and gets flippant, and the worrywarts tell you that your child must be on drugs or in a gang (or both). You lose your job and they dump the world on your shoulders and convince you that if you get another job, it won't be for 12 to 18 months minimum, and you will most likely take a huge pay cut. You have been trying a few months to get pregnant, you make the mistake of mentioning this to a worrywart. This person then blows things out of proportion and now is fixated on the probability of you and/or your spouse being infertile, and your inability to conceive.

Your loved one is in the military and you haven't heard from them in months, the worrywarts have told you of a possible MIA, POW situation—they start planting the seed that you may need to start planning a memorial. Your business isn't where you had hoped it would be, they tell you to stop while you're ahead and go get a job. A doctor tells you that he/she has found a lump in your breast, growth in your cervix, an abnormality in your lungs, or growth in your prostate. The worrywarts have diagnosed you with full-blown cancer with zero chances of recovery, and a life expectancy of less than a few months. They cry on your shoulder and start going down memory lane with you, already "digging" your grave.

Stay away from these people. If they are family, then limit what you share with them, and how much time you spend with them. Surround yourself with people who are more like Peter, James, and his brother John. Surround yourself with true believers, faith walkers, the Lydia's who jump right in without question, the commitment and boldness of Esther. Even in your fear and lack of faith, those who believe will help push you through. Those who believe will bring in the energy and light needed for you to fixate only on God and not on the problem. Is it dead or is it asleep, and just needs to be awakened? It is what you believe.

NOTES

Day 233: Don't Let FOMO Get You Caught Up

GO DEEPER!

As an adult I have tried to leave even my worst adversary with their dignity, agreeing to disagree, and agreeing that the best solution at times is to walk away and let God deal with it without our interference. I refuse to "kick" someone while they are down, and I refuse to "strip" someone of their perceived worth for my gain. Although I always want the truth revealed, I will not fight with the purpose and goal of tearing someone else down. God's Truth is always revealed, right on time. My efforts won't necessarily speed up the process, and especially if my motives are not pure. In that case, the process will always be slowed to a crawl, because it is then no longer about God, and mostly about me.

Have you noticed this process in your life? Have you noticed that even when trying to do good, if a large part of your motivation is for yourself, the process is delayed and oftentimes bumpy? All things good must be done with God as the foundation, source, motivation, and reason. The feeling of achieving that should outweigh any awards and accolades that man could ever bestow upon you. I serve for Him, not for me. I give for Him, not for me. I live for Him not for me. Each day I say and give thanks for the breath that I take because it is God's will and grace that blesses me with another day to serve as He sees fit. I can't take the awards and human recognition with me to the next level of existence, but I can take the feelings and warmth received from each person who I touched directly and indirectly. I can embrace God's love and forgiveness. That my friends— is priceless!

NOTES

Day 234: Reach Out in Obedience

GO DEEPER!

1. Review what you wrote on Day 204. What have you committed to?
2. What challenges have you faced over the past 30 days?
3. Review what you wrote on Day 207. What progress have you made towards your goals?
4. How does that make you feel?
5. Which of the dreams that you wrote about are forming more clearly in your mind?

Remain focused on what God has promised you. Reach out to Him in obedience.

NOTES

Day 235: Throw Stones Your Way

GO DEEPER!

We have used the Bible to condone slavery, abuse of women and children, rape, murder, the start of wars, racism, sexism, classism, pedophilia, robbing church members of their hard-earned money so that we can build bigger and flashier churches, and place our so-called religious leaders in fancier homes and cars—while paying them millions to do what Jesus and his disciples did for free.

We are fortunate to have God's grace upon us this day because He could easily wipe us out like Sodom and Gomorrah, or worse, like the great flood (where he only spared Noah, his immediate family, and two of each animal and creature) and start over from scratch.

We should stand up and speak out against those who victimize, take advantage of, and snatch the purity away from others. We should embrace those who mutually love, uplift, restore, and empower others. The adult couple who love each other and cause no harm to others, should not be judged by us. If God does not approve of their relationship, that is His situation to deal with. Do we think that He can't handle it? Do we think that we can resolve things better and faster than He? We have our problems and our sins we must deal with and atone for, get out of other people's business, especially if their issues aren't negatively impacting others.

NOTES

Day 236: His Faithfulness Endures Forever

GO DEEPER!

1. What would you like to thank God for today?
2. How strong is your faith (support in) God today?
3. Have you been going through anything that has been testing your faith? If so, what?

Pray for God's intervention, protection, and care.

NOTES

Day 237: Hope Defined

GO DEEPER!
1. What do you hope for?
2. Why?

NOTES

Day 238: Growing in God's Grace

GO DEEPER!

We must change to grow. We should want the change and do our part to change. We should desire to grow in God's grace. Sadly, many of us grow the hard way and in doing so, we may not gain the knowledge to learn the lessons we need. You have to want it.

NOTES

Day 239: What Prophecy Is NOT

GO DEEPER!

It is said that a prophecy is spoken by a prophet inspired by God to speak a prediction or statement by God. To prophesy is to predict or make a statement about something inspired by God. However, we know that many people utter words not inspired or commanded by God. People have said, "God told me..." and they expect you to believe them without question, just because they lead with that statement.

Don't be fooled with titles and people professing to be someone or something. Jesus taught the people that his time on the cross would position us to speak and hear directly from God. Yes, some people are more gifted, they seem like conduits but beware of relying upon others to communicate messages to and from God— you could easily be misled.

NOTES

Day 240: Supplement Faith

GO DEEPER!

Reflecting over today's message, what are you using as layers to supplement your faith?

NOTES

Day 241: Your Protector Never Sleeps

GO DEEPER!

In what ways can you lean more on God and rely upon Him for protection and provision?

NOTES

Day 242: Fact-Checking and Truth Speaking

GO DEEPER!

1. What doubts do you have in your life? Why?
2. Go to God with these doubts. The longer you hold on to them the more the enemy deceives and confuses you.
3. Write on a piece of paper the things you are dealing with but you're doubting that there will be a positive and fast resolution. Write today's date on it and then put it in your "For God" container. You can also use the free downloadable sheets located at DOMELifePublishing.com

NOTES

Day 243: Death Destroyed

GO DEEPER!

1. When you look around your city, state, country, and the world do you see more sinners or more people doing good and trying to be redeemed?
2. Do you think this is accurate or just your perception? Why?
3. Do you think that sin was a greater issue in Jesus' time or now? Why?
4. Do you feel discouraged or encouraged by the word declaring God's victory over sin and death? Why?
5. In what ways can you live your life with a victory mindset so that today is better than yesterday, and tomorrow can be better than today?

NOTES

Day 244: What Is Most Important in Your Life?

GO DEEPER!

1. Reflect over the last several months. Which areas have you grown most? Least?
2. What is most important to you in your life? Why?
3. Keep focused on your mission, purpose, goals, and dreams that you shared on Days 204 and 207. Retrieve that list and reflect over them.
4. What do you visualize in your mind when you see this list? How do you feel about pursuing and one day achieving these things?
5. How are you serving as the barrier/blockage that is slowing your progress?
6. What do you want God to assist you with so that you can be all that He created you to be?

NOTES

GREATER CONTEXT

Abram/Abraham

Abram's name in Hebrew means "exalted father". He was from the city of Ur Kasdim (translated as the Ur of the Chaldeans) in Mesopotamia, which was a well-to-do city. He was an Aramean (just like Noah) which means that he and his people spoke Aramaic. Before his journey with God, his family, like most Arameans of that time, were polytheists who worshiped Mesopotamian gods and Canaanite-Phoenician deities. This is why he built an altar to God as his sign of commitment, as altar-building (especially with one or more stones) was a custom in "primitive" religions, long before adopted as a practice in Judaism and later Christianity. God met Abram where he was in his life, understanding that his people had a different reference point for who and how they worshiped. You will see this throughout the Bible, that is why God appeared in different ways and forms and had His angels appear in different forms and ways, depending on how the person that they visited was spiritually rooted.

If you paid close attention to his family tree, Abram's father was Terah and his mother was Edna. His grandfather was Nahor I and his 9th great grandfather was Shem, whose father was Noah (Abram's 10th great grandfather). Abram had two other brothers, Nahor II (named after their grandfather) and Haran, who died and left behind three children: Lot, Iscah, and daughter Milcah (who Nahor II later married). Sarai is Abram's wife and step-sister (she is the daughter of Terah whose mother was not Abram's mother).

If you recall, Abram and Sarai were living with Terah, along with Lot (Haran's son). It's obvious that Nahor II had already married Milcah and lived on his own, and Iscah was either married off or just wasn't seen as relevant to the storyline to share more details about her— because when Terah packed up and moved the family to the land of Haran, only Terah, Lot, Abram, Sarai, and the servants of Terah made the trip. This would lead you to believe that Abram and Sarai were still not old enough to live on their own. It seems that once Abram reached the age of maturity, that is when God called on him to pack up and hit the road with Sarai and Lot [Genesis 12]. Abram is the first of God's faithful wanderers, pilgrims, journeymen. God calls on Abram to leave his home, his family and friends, and all that is familiar to him, and go to an unspecified destination, trusting God along the way. God leads him to the land of Canaan (that was established by Abram's 9th great cousin and son of Ham) to the town of Shechem [Gen.12:6-7]. Yes, the same Canaan that established the Canaanites mentioned earlier. You have to know the story of Canaan to understand why his land would be promised by God to Abram's line. Read the section on Noah in this chapter to learn more.

God's covenant with Abram was to make a great nation from his lineage and make his name great so that he would be a blessing to others. A man's name represented their reputation, one of honor or dishonor. Abram didn't ask God a bunch of questions, he didn't object, he simply went. He trusted and obeyed. The Kingdom of God started with a journey. If you think about it, most of the Bible's heroes were pilgrims. They weren't rooted long-term anywhere. They would pitch their tents and move from place to place. Ironically or best-suiting, ancient Jews referred to their bodies as tents, as a form of symbolism.

Tower of Babel

It is said that the Kingdom of God is found on the road, not in or on the tower, like the Babylonians tried to do by building a "tower to the heaven and let us make a name for ourselves" [Gen.11:4]. The Tower of Babel is said to be a symbol of what's wrong with religion, why Jesus despised religion so much: when humans decided to do for themselves without God, building their own stairway to heaven, being driven by ego, pride, and greed. Babel first meant "Gateway to God" in Hebrew and now it means "Confusion". Man can't build up to God by his own work. Interestingly, Shem's genealogy is mentioned after the story of Nimrod and the Babylonians' Tower, because God was building His Kingdom through Noah's son Shem's line, with one man, not a bunch of bricks —like the Tower of Babel. We're so distracted by building man's kingdoms when we should be helping God with His Kingdom. Instead of trying to get to heaven, let's help God keep His promise to bring heaven to Earth.

Abram/Abraham's Lack of Trust

We can learn a lot from studying Abram's life and how he later was renamed Abraham "father of many" [Gen.17:5]. Although God looked at him and saw genuine faith that he credited as righteousness [Gen.15:6] we know that Abram/Abraham had plenty of flaws and fears. He and Sarai didn't fully trust Him to keep His promise to give them a son, so they jumped the gun and had Sarai's Egyptian handmaid, Hagar, birth a son (Ishmael) with Abram [Genesis 16]. That got messy real fast and proved why God didn't approve of bigamy. Abram/Abraham feared dying so he kept sacrificing, in a way, his wife Sarai (later renamed Sarah by God in Genesis 17:15) to avoid being killed by men who Abram/Abraham feared would desire her so much that they would try to take her from him and kill him to speed up the process.

There wasn't enough trust in God to consult Him first. Instead, Abram/Abraham would say Sarai/Sarah was his sister (not his wife) and hand her over in exchange for money, animals, etc. He let the men take Sarai/Sarah with no plan of getting her back, and no real consideration as to what would happen to her. There is a term for this, but I won't say it here. But you know what I'm talking about, don't you? Both times this happened, God had to intervene to get her back. Read Genesis 12 and Genesis 20 to see how Abram/Abraham kept messing that up, and see how this fear and lack of trust is also tested later on in his son Isaac. We can also learn how we too screw up when our fear gets in the way and faith takes a backseat.

How Are You Like Abram?

God needed Abram/Abraham to be separate and set apart from everyone and everything else. He said he brought Abram out of his old life in Ur to bring him to greatness [Gen.15:7] and fulfill a purpose. What has God promised you? What is He trying to set you apart from so that He can bring you to greatness? Abram said he needed reassurance, a sign [Gen.15:8]. Don't we often ask

God for a sign, some level of proof that what He's promised will be ours? To align with Abram's traditions and customs, God told him they would "cut covenant", collecting and cutting in half all of the animals (except the birds) to be sacrificed [Gen.15:8-10]. This was to prove the seriousness of the agreement. Like, how later, when people would cut their hands and shake in agreement. Or when you were growing up and you did spit handshakes. Now most of us use written contracts and involve lawyers in big agreements. But how are we supposed to handle our faith walk when we want a sign of assurance from God?

In 2 Corinthians 5:7, we're taught that "...we live by faith, not by sight" and so we don't do cut covenants and we're not supposed to ask for signs. We're supposed to believe based on all of the blessings that God has already given us. If you continued reading Genesis 15, then you know that God didn't remove his halves of the animals, as what would be traditionally done. God blessed Abram with His grace, expecting nothing in return—no conditions. God has promised us an abundance of blessings; He's waiting for us to act through obedience, even into the unknown.

His Wives

Sarah passed away in Hebron [Gen. 23:1]. At some point, Abraham remarried and his new wife, Keturah, gave birth to six sons: Zimran, Jokshan (who had two children and three grandchildren), Medan, Midian (who had five sons and became the Midianites), Ishbak, and Shuah. Abraham left gifts for his son Ishmael (who had a daughter and 12 sons who all became princes) and for his six sons with Keturah, but he gave everything he owned to Isaac. Some Jewish commentators believe that Keturah is Hagar; that the name Hagar means "stranger" (since she was Egyptian) but that her given name was Keturah, and they believe that Abraham remarried her and had the six sons together[1]. Others agree that they are the same, but that the name Keturah is the descriptor and not the given name[2]. We may never know, one thing that we do know is that Abraham was still fathering children in his well-seasoned age.

Altars

Did you find it interesting that the first time the use of an altar in the Bible is mentioned when Noah built one for God [Gen.8:20]? The other times were Abraham [Gen.12:7,13:4, 22:9], Isaac [Gen. 26:25], Jacob [Gen.33:20, 35:1-3], and Moses [Ex.17:15]. Then one was erected after the theophany on Mount Sinai in the Tabernacle, and afterward, in the Temple in Jerusalem, there were two altars used: Altar of Burnt Offering and Altar of Incense. The Greek word for altar appears 24 times in the New Testament, but there aren't any stories shared with the specificity of the Old Testament. The earliest altars probably originated when certain trees, rocks, springs, etc. were regarded as holy or as being inhabited by a spirit or god whose intervention could be solicited by the worshiper. As mentioned earlier in the Abram/Abraham summary, a lot of primitive religions used a stone, heap of stones, or a mound of earth for this purpose. Just like when Jacob used a stone that he poured oil on, naming it Beth-El "House of El" (House of God).

With the development of a formalized institution of sacrifice in sanctuaries and temples, the altars became more elaborate looking, being built of stone or brick for sacrifices. The blood channeled off or its flesh burned. Altars in other parts of the Middle East ranged from small stands that were upright and used for burning incense, and then there were some large rectangular ones made out of stone, such as the ones built by the Egyptians for their temples (during the New Kingdom period). Remember, Egyptians are descendants from Noah's grandson Misraim (which means "Egypt" in English) the son of Ham.

Early Christians didn't use altars or temples in worship. They started using a table that was regarded as an altar to celebrate the Eucharist (Holy Communion/Lord's Supper) by the 3rd century AD. By the time they began building churches, Christians also started using wooden altar tables in the area where the choir was. Does it feel strange to you to know that the altar at the front of your church has ties to the ancient sacrificial altars of primitive religions? Be sure to read the section on "Human Sacrifices" in this chapter. It's interesting how many things and practices (past and present) that we find in Judaism and Christianity are a mishmash of other religions.

Angel of the Lord

Maybe you haven't noticed, or maybe you have—there is one particular angel mentioned in the Old Testament, but never mentioned with a name, and represented in some translations with the letter "A" in angel capitalized. This angel was called "The Angel of God" and "The Angel of the Lord". Other translations say "The Messenger" instead of Angel and that is because angels were seen as God's messengers. Some commentators and scholars believe that this Angel/Messenger was and is Jesus. When we read of other accounts of angels in the Bible, they are always mentioned by name, such as Gabriel [Luke 1:19]. One of the arguments that The Angel is not just a regular angel, is that The Angel of the Lord is the only angel that appeared and referred to himself as the Lord and God in the first person. All of the other angels mentioned always referred to God in the third person, and they humbled themselves refusing to take any glory or be worshiped. Also, this angel is not mentioned ever in the New Testament, and it is said that the reason for that is because Jesus was here in human form[3]. Let's look at a few specific examples of the Angel of the Lord and Angel of God as mentioned in the Bible:

- Genesis 16:7-14: The Angel of the Lord appears to Hagar and speaks in the first person as God himself
- Genesis 22:11-15: The Angel of the Lord appeared to Abraham and referred to himself in the first person as God
- Exodus 3:2-4: The Angel of the Lord appears to Moses in a flame (speaking in the first person) and in verse 4, God speaks in the first person to Moses through the flame
- Numbers 22:22-38: The Angel of the Lord meets the prophet Balaam on the road
- Zechariah 1:12: The Angel of the Lord pleads with the Lord to have mercy on Jerusalem and the cities of Judah
- Zechariah 3:4: The Angel of the Lord takes away the sin of the high priest Joshua

- Judges 13:9-22: The Angel of God came to Manoah's wife and she runs to her husband telling him "He's here, the man who appeared to me the other day" and then the Angel of the Lord engaged in a conversation with Manoah. The Angel also ascended into the altar's fire and when he didn't return, Manoah knew the man "was the Angel of the Lord". He then thought they were going to die because "We have seen God".
- Genesis 31:11: The Angel of God calls out to Jacob in a dream, "I am the God of Bethel"
- Exodus 14:19: The Angel of God leads the camp of Israel, and follows behind them with the pillar of fire
- Exodus 23: 20-21: God says He was sending an Angel before the Israelites and He warned that they needed to obey the Angel, and that the Angel would not "pardon transgressions" because the LORD'S "name is in him".

It is believed by some that the Angel of the Lord/God prefigures the reconciling ministry of Jesus. While others believe that Jesus helped God with the creation phases of Genesis, but that he only came to Earth as the Messiah, and that somehow being an angel would be a rank below him[4] But if people can wrap their minds around God transforming to ranks "below him" to come to Earth, why can't they fathom God sending instead, Jesus, as his spiritual self? Could you not see how it could be possible that it was decided that Jesus would need to be fully immersed as a human to save us, for only through our connection and ability to relate to him as another human, could we then feel qualified to follow him? We wouldn't be able to relate to an angelic being, as there are several examples of how humans responded when they realized they were in the presence of an angel. It was too much for them to handle. God had to send a more relatable example to follow.

Does that make sense to you?

What are your thoughts on this? Did God just send any ole' angel? Did He send a special angel whose name remained a secret? Did He decide to personally pop down in a form that clearly left the impression of being an angel? Or do you think that it's more probable that Jesus, His Messenger, made frequent appearances to numerous people as The Angel until eventually, God told him it was time to ramp up their efforts? I can see a conversation that was sort of like this:

"They're crying out to Me for a King, so let's give them one they can follow back to Me. You will need to be fully immersed in the human experience, birthed by a human mother, you will labor, and feel the restrictions of the flesh so that you can experience their life and understand their struggles. Then you can teach them and show them how to overcome Satan's traps and return to My Kingdom".

It's something to ponder and consider!

Christian Denominations and Complex Belief Systems

A lot of what you believe about your religion and other religions is based on what someone taught you in church or school. It's usually not from your independent exploration of the topics and practices. What we know as Christianity today is a hodgepodge of other philosophies and practices that attempt to focus on and around one savior, Jesus Christ, and on one God (called by many names). In the 16th century, Protestants tried to distinguish themselves and protest some of the tenants and formalities of the Roman Catholic church, however, some of the influences of the Roman culture and Catholic church are still ironically interwoven in the Protestant belief system, including the tendency to be historical and cultural revisionists. And if you're saying, "But Catholics aren't Christians" then I'm gonna need you to do your research. They are the largest denomination of Christianity, making up more than 50 percent, with Protestants making up roughly 37 percent. If you identify as a Christian but not as Catholic, and you were raised in the U.S. then you're most likely a Protestant—which are the Baptists, Anglicans, Lutherans, Calvinists, Methodists, Pentecostals, Quakers, Seventh-Day Adventists, Hussites, Nondenominatialists, Messianic Judaists, etc. That leaves the rest of the religious "pie" to Eastern/Oriental Orthodox Christians (roughly 12%) and 1.2 percent of people who identify as "Other Christian". Check out the archives of the Pew Forum for more information[5] So whichever box you check and choose to fit in just understand that the framework of your beliefs was slowly molded from thought systems that chose to pivot from the early ancient Judeo-Christian thought.

Christmas

Christians have been celebrating December 25th as the anniversary of Jesus' birth. December 25th has been a federally recognized holiday in the US since 1870. But is December 25th Jesus' birthday? In the early days of Christianity, Easter was the main holiday celebrated. No one celebrated Jesus' birthday. In the fourth century, church officials decided to make his birthday a holiday. But they weren't sure how since the Bible never mentioned a date of birth. It was argued that it was most likely during the spring season since shepherds wouldn't be herding sheep in winter. But Pope Julius I selected December 25th. But why?

For centuries before the birth of Jesus, early Europeans celebrated the winter solstice, as it was the time when the harsh weather was ending and they could enjoy longer days and more sunlight. The winter solstice begins December 21st and the Norse people in Scandanavia celebrated the Yule holiday from December 21st through January. The men would bring home large logs and set them on fire and there would be daily feasts until the logs burned out, which was usually 12 days. They believed that every spark and flame of the fire represented the births of new calves and pigs in the New Year. December was the perfect time to celebrate Yule because usually the ale and wine they were fermenting throughout the year were ready by end-of-year. Also, most cattle had been slaughtered, so there was plenty of food, and for many people in Europe, this was the only time when they had fresh meat in the year. By the 1600s the inclusion of Yule log cakes brought chocolate sweetness and yumminess to tables all over. To this day, people enjoy eating Yule log cakes. You have probably eaten one and didn't know its history. Well, now you do.

In Germany, they worshiped the god Oden and they believed that during the mid-winter holiday, Ogden would fly over their homes at night to judge who would prosper or perish in the new year. In Rome, they had a holiday that started the week before the winter solstice. It was called Saturnalia. They didn't have harsh winters like those farther north, so they celebrated for an entire month. They were hedonists who enjoyed drinking, eating, and taking part in flipping the traditional Roman order upside down. During this holiday they practiced role reversal, where the enslaved were the masters, and peasants were in control of the city. All schools and businesses would be closed for the entire month. Around the Winter Solstice, they would have a feast, Juvenalia, that honored the Roman children. The upper echelon of society also celebrated the birthday of Mithra, the "god of the unconquerable sun". Mithra's birthday was December 25th. They believed Mithra was born of a rock and was an infant god. Some Romans saw this day as the most sacred day of the year.

Now can you guess why Pope Julius I selected December 25th?

It is said that he did this to adopt and absorb the traditions of the Saturnalia festival. First called the Feast of Nativity, this festival spread to Egypt by 432, and by the end of the sixth century, it had reached England. Since it was being held at the same time as the Winter Solstice festivals it would be more easily recognized and embraced. Church leaders gave up on trying to dictate how Christmas would be embraced. They just wanted to blot out the other festivals. By the Middle Ages, Christianity had almost completely replaced pagan religions. Christmas day in that era was seen as the day to attend church then get skunky drunk at their carnival-like celebrations, like a wild night at Mardi Gras. They also borrowed some of the traditions of Saturnalia by having students or beggars play the "lord of the misrule" and people would pretend to be the lord's subjects. The poor could go to the houses of the wealthy and demand food and drink, and terrorize them if they didn't comply. This was the time of the year when the wealthy paid a "debt" of service by entertaining the poor.

In the early 17th century there was a major overhaul to Christmas throughout Europe. The Puritans, led by Oliver Cromwell, took over the leadership of England in 1645 and vowed to do away with the foolishness, and they went about canceling Christmas. Is this the first cancel culture recorded? Just kidding. Well when Charles II was restored to the throne, Christmas was restored to the people of England. It hadn't made it to the Americas though. The pilgrims were more orthodox than the Puritans, so there was no way they were bringing Christmas with them to this new country. It was outlawed in Boston from 1659 to 1681. People were fined if caught celebrating Christmas. But in Jamestown, it was celebrated freely.

After the American Revolution, nobody wanted to take part in English traditions, which included Christmas. Not until the 19th century, when it was re-invented and morphed into a family-centered day of peace, joy, and being caught up in those nostalgic memories of the past. High unemployment and rioting by gangs caused a lot of turmoil and trauma throughout the land and it occurred mostly during the wintertime. The rowdy Christmas partying of the past had led to riots and stupidity, so the upper class took it upon themselves to reinvent Christmas. With the publishing of various books by Washington Irving (1819) and Charles Dickens [A Christmas Carol], Americans began to refocus their attention on family and most pointedly on lavishing gifts on their oftentimes neglected children, without spoiling them. For 100 years, Americans began to adopt traditions and customs from newly-arrived immigrants, Catholic churches, and Episcopalian churches. They incorporated tree decorating, gift-giving, and sending of holiday cards.

In the late 18th century, New Yorkers blended in the concept of Santa Clause, which was taken from the story of the Turkish monk, St. Nicholas, who was born around 280 AD, and he gave away his inheritance, traveling around to help the sick and poor. The people called him the protector of children and sailors. In New York, the Dutch families would come together to honor his death. They called him Sint Nikolaas or Sinter Klass for short. That's where we got St. Nick and Santa Claus. Twas The Night Before Christmas was a poem written in 1822 by the Episcopal minister, Clement Clarke Moore. Then our imagery of Santa was locked in and deeply embedded when political cartoonist Thomas Nast drew an image of Saint Nick in 1881, using the words from minister Moore's poem. That cartoon is the image we have held onto ever since.[6]

Comparing Adam to Jesus

If you recall from SEEK HIM, Volume 1, I explained that in Hebrew, Adam (HaAdam) is translated as man (The Man). It was not his name but rather his defined gender or identity as part of the human species. Yes, there are other words for man (ish) and woman (isha), but about these specific people, their creation by God directly and not through seed formation (as God blesses most of His creations), we understand who is being referenced when the names Adam and Eve (Chavah) are used. This distinguishes them from all others.

After Adam fell into temptation, God cursed him, and told him that he was made of dust and would return to it when he died [Gen. 3:19]; which means that was never the initial plan for humans. They were to live forever. Genesis 1 and Genesis 2 show how God intended for us to be and Genesis 3 shows what humans chose to become. It is said that Adam is the first man and Jesus is the last man. Scientifically, we know that Adam, as told in the Bible, is not the first man, if you follow the genealogical tree from Adam to Jesus, and then look at the calendar through today. What I mean by this is, we have human remains that are more than 300,000 years old. You can do the math and see when Adam was created. So one can argue that the Bible is solely the Genesis (beginning) and a story of one ethnic-religious group of people (with small peeks into other groups). It's quite understandable to wrap your mind around the concept of God starting over multiple times, just as He is said to have done with the great flood in which He spared Noah, his wife, sons, and their wives.

Is it possible that Adam and Eve (Chavah) did not truly comprehend the meaning of death when God told them they would "surely die" from eating the "fruit" from the Tree? Yes. But, they found out eventually, when they both died. They made a stupid decision that separated them from God and destroyed their union as partners (since part of the curse was that now the husband would rule over her instead of with her).

Let's compare Adam to Jesus:

Adam— backed off and caved in, followed Eve's lead (or at least, chose to be in alignment), didn't ask questions, didn't counter-argue, didn't go and consult God.

Jesus— was steadfast, always took the lead, always questioned, always counter-argued, and always consulted God through prayer and meditation.

Adam— took no responsibility for his actions, blamed God for giving him Eve, and then blamed Eve.

Jesus— took all of the blame, always took responsibility, was accountable for his words and actions.

Adam— gave into temptation, listened to Satan, sinned, fell from a place of glory and honor.

Jesus— never gave into temptation, told Satan to kick rocks, never sinned, and laid down his life to redeem the fallen man, to stand once again.

Adam— caused the curse.

Jesus— will reverse the curse through the destruction of sin and Satan.

Adam— created by God without a mother, lived, reproduced, experienced hard labor, and died an old man.

Jesus— created by God, birthed through a human mother, no known offspring, experienced persecution, was crucified and resurrected, and then he ascended.

Both Adam and Eve were described before the fall as having skin that was "luminous", divine light, glowing— which is how the angels, Moses, and Messiah were described. After the fall that divine light is covered. We too walk around covered, waiting to be freed so that our luminous glow can be revealed. To ensure that sin is blotted out, Satan is defeated, and the curse is reversed, we have to do our part:

- To only be led by God and consult Him always,
- Take responsibility for our actions,
- Don't give in to temptation,
- Stop sinning,
- Be obedient and faithful to God, realign with Him, and worship only Him,
- Use things and not people, and
- Fix our marriages to reflect His original plan of an equal and respectful partnership.

Easter

For Christians, Easter is the celebration of Jesus' resurrection. Jesus was sentenced to death by Pontius Pilate, the Roman prefect (from 26 to 36 AD) in the province of Judea. Jesus' crucifixion was Good Friday, the Friday before Easter. His resurrection was three days later.

Although this is our modern-day celebration of Jesus, many of the traditions we practice have absolutely no connection to the Bible. Easter was a pagan holiday that serves as the start of the season of Pascha, which is Greek for "Easter", in Eastern Orthodox branches of Christianity. Many traditions and symbols of Easter observances have roots in pagan celebrations:

- The pagan goddess Eostre (or Ostara)
- Ancient Germanic goddess of spring

The Easter Bunny came from German immigrants who came to America in the 1700s and brought their tradition and stories of an egg-laying hare, Osterhase to the state of Pennsylvania. Egg decorating began around the 13th century, and the children would place the eggs in nests. So of course they would bring this tradition to America. The Easter bunny and egg tradition spread throughout the U.S. It evolved to include chocolate, candies, and gifts, and the nests were replaced with baskets. Rabbits are known for cranking out babies like crazy, so they have carried an ancient symbol of fertility and new life. Eggs also symbolize fertility and new life. Eggs have a history of being associated with pagan festivals when celebrating Spring. The decorating of eggs dates back to the 13th century when people would paint and decorate them to mark the end of penance and fasting tied to the Lenten season. On Easter, they would eat the eggs in celebration.

Lamb is a traditional food of choice at Easter, with it representing Christ as the lamb of God. Lamb also has roots in early Passover celebrations. Historically, a lamb would be one of the first fresh meats available to eat after a long winter with no livestock to slaughter. Springtime meant people could finally eat some fresh meat[7]. This once again reinforces that Jesus wasn't born in December or at any time in the winter, because the shepherds wouldn't have been out in the fields with their flock. But we can still choose to celebrate Jesus' birth on December 25th since it does make us feel good during the time of year where winter days get tough.

Evolutionists Can't Explain...

Here's something to think about, as shared by Kris Langham from the Through The Word ministry: Evolutionists can't explain gravity, water, light, and magnetism. It wasn't until the 16th century AD that scientists understood the water cycle, yet the Bible describes it accurately in the 9th century BC [Job 36 and Ecc. 1]. Evolutionists talk about a microorganism that evolved and eventually was a water species that made it to land, kept evolving, became an ape, then over time transitioned into a human. But evolutionists can't explain reproduction. How could the first creature reproduce? Just something to think about!

Gnosticism

Not to be confused with Agnosticism (which is the view that the belief in God or a Supernatural Being existing is unknown or unknowable), the word Gnosticism is ancient Greek for "having knowledge". We touched on this in Seek Him: Workbook 1. Gnosticism is a collection or culmination of religious systems and ideas that originated in the first century AD amongst early Jewish sects and Christians[8]. When you research and study Gnosticism you see the influences of Zoroastrianism, Buddhism, Platonism (inspired by some of the philosophic beliefs of Plato), Hinduism, and Hellenistic Judaism. We explored these briefly in Seek Him: Workbook 1.

You would be surprised how much Christianity has in common with Gnosticism than most conservative Christians would like to admit. For some odd reason, Christians tend to believe that the concepts, systems, and ideas of Christianity are all original thoughts and exclusive of all others. As I shared in my previous Seek Him books, Christianity is a blend of early religious thoughts, principles, and practices. Some of you may cringe and scream, "I rebuke that in the Name of Jesus" and that is fine, but that also just reinforces the fact that you too haven't researched the roots and foundational principles and concepts of the religion called Christianity. Most likely, you are standing on what you were taught in Sunday school and church, and you never explored beyond what was told to you. This Seek Him book series is challenging you to do more, read more, see more, ask more, and be more. So if you're ready, continue reading.

Gnosticism focuses on personal spiritual knowledge over orthodox traditions and teachings. It goes against the perceived authority that the church says it has over us. Gnostics believe in our personal relationship and connection with God, and that we have the personal power and capability to reach out and strengthen that connection. Basically, we don't need the church or a leader of the church to be our intermediary.

Hmmm, who else taught us that? Jesus!

Do you remember how outraged the religious leaders were at Jesus for telling people that they could go directly to God, speak directly to God, possess the same power and capabilities that he (Jesus) possesses—if only the people believed and chose to tap into that Source? Well, we all know how that turned out for Jesus and the disciples and apostles that continued practicing and teaching this for hundreds of years after his ascension. In Gnosticism, there is a greater focus on people as spiritual beings, looking more toward enlightenment and salvation coming in the form of having direct knowledge of the Supreme Deity, that many of us call God/Yahweh/Jehovah. While Christians speak of sin and repentance, Gnostics speak of illusion and enlightenment. There is a sole focus on the spirit while modern Christians are heavily focused on the flesh. Early Christians were mostly spiritual-based and over the past several hundred years there has been a greater focus on our humanness and why we need our church leaders to help be the bridge to God and Jesus, for us to be saved.

If you want to know why your church's leadership speaks so negatively about Gnosticism (and the other religious systems that are blended within this system) you can thank two sources:

1. Ignorance—simply not knowing because they don't study and seek answers, and so they speak from not knowing (and as I mentioned in the beginning, some may be confusing it with Agnosticism), and
2. Arrogance drives the opinion that "my way is the only and best way" and that "I know best"—which is dogmatism at its worst and best.

Let us not forget that early Christianity was molded by Judaism (as Jesus and his early followers were Jews) and ancient Rome (as the Jews were under Roman rule). This molding blended in politics with culture and religion. Those early Romans evolved into what we now see as the driving force of the Roman Catholic and Eastern Orthodox churches, which renounce any ideas and ways that differ their views. It is also what causes many Christians to speak and behave dogmatically and with great divisiveness—which is both alarming and frightening.

And this renouncement is fueled by ignorance or quite possibly, knowing the truth, but choosing an alternative way because they prefer their way. Do you recall the ulterior motives of the religious leaders and scholars who omitted ancient text from being included in the Old Testament and later the New Testament? I mean, heck, rather than omit them they could have been combined into separate texts for our study, but instead, they made the decision for us. Just as many translators decided to translate Hebrew and Aramaic into what they wanted the text to say, and completely skewed the context of the ancient beliefs, culture, and history. Hence why I decided to include the "Ponder This, Consider That" and "Greater Context" sections in my Seek Him book series. We shouldn't continue operating from a blindspot.

God: Polytheism Revisited

Let's revisit the idea of polytheism in ancient Judaism before it was organized religion. Before the Temple was destroyed and the people were exiled in 586 B.C., the ancient Israelites were polytheists. Because they had the nomadic influences of other beliefs, cultures, religions, and norms, that blend helped to shape their views and how they worshiped. It wasn't until after 586 B.C. that a teeny tiny cluster of Israelites began to focus on a monotheistic, one God, belief system. But they didn't go around calling themselves "monotheists". Around 5 B.C. you begin to see a shift in the writing within the Hebrew Bible, where God is mentioned in the singular and not the plural. Even in 70 CE when the Romans conquered Jerusalem, most people weren't aligned with a one-God way of life. It wasn't until around the 4th century A.D. that the concept of a singular God even appeared in Christian writings. The majority didn't begin to join in until a form of voting took place during the era of Constantine (when he was trying to unify the Romans and Christians and made the bold decision to declare the land Christian-ruled). Even after that, there was a lot of flip-flopping and arguing going on and finally church leaders agreed on "there's only one God, our God". And let's be clear, this was also the same awkward transition for Islam as if you read the Quran you can see the use of the plural in reference to Allah ("God" in Arabic).

So let's look at a few examples in the Bible, shall we? If you recall, in Seek Him, Volume 1 and Workbook 1, I challenged you to research the "Priestly Authors" who penned Genesis and other writings. Look at how they referred to God and recorded His statements—not as a singular Being. I will provide you with the Hebrew and English words so that you have as much context as possible.

In Genesis 1:26 it says "let Us make man in Our tzelem (image), after Our demut (likeness)...".

In Genesis 3:22 it says, "And the Name of God said, See, the man (HaAdam) is become like one of Us (ke-achad mimmmennu), knowing good and evil (tov v'rah)".

When God noticed that the people could achieve their goal of reaching Heaven with their Tower, He said "let Us go down" [Genesis 11:7] there, separate them, and confuse them with different languages.

Also, throughout the Old Testament, God is oftentimes referred to as Elohim, which is the plural form of God. It is now said that Elohim can refer to a single deity or the plural form of Eloah. It is related to El, which also means God in Hebrew and Aramaic. It's not surprising that early believers would consider a plural concept, since they had a history of worshiping multiple deities and gods before, during, and after the times of Moses. Even if Elohim was used to refer to one God, then who is the "Us" and the "Our" mentioned in Genesis and other parts of the Bible? Some people say it's God and Jesus. Others say it's just a misquoting of God.

Well, another controversial position is the belief that the Genesis 1 account of God making male and female simultaneously, was the act of a male God and female God, like husband and wife (which then supports God's reasoning for wanting the man to also have a wife). Even the Genesis 2 account of God making a female equal for the male, supports the idea that the reference of a female would come from Him having His equal in feminine form. Some people who believe this also believe that the female goddess Asherah is the female partner of God. She is God's wife, so to speak. Before you throw this book against the wall or into a fire pit, please keep reading. In the Book of Kings, we read of the people worshiping both Yahweh/Jehovah and Asherah in the temple in Israel. Asherah was/is a fertility goddess. If your translated Bible version does not mention her by name then you can thank the editors for blotting her out and most likely inserting in a reference to a sacred tree. If your Bible version mentions a sacred tree or tries to convince you that the name of the tree is Asherah, like an Oak or Pine tree, please know that this is historical and cultural revisionism to blot out the mention of the goddess Asherah.

Now if that didn't make your wig or toupe' spin and fall lopsided, let me share some other long-held thoughts. While many others strongly believe that although there is one Supreme God, the Almighty God (El Shaddai), that there are some periphery gods that make up His counsel. Judaism is not the only religion that mentions a type of Divine Council or Divine Assembly. You also read of it in ancient Canaanite [Noah's grandson Canaan's line], ancient Greek, Rome, Egyptian [Noah's grandson Misraim's line], and Babylonian [Noah's grandson Nimrod's line]. There are also tie-ins found in Chinese theology, Norse, Celtic mythology, and other groups. In the Bible, read Psalms 82, 1 Kings 22, and Job 1 and Job 2.

What do you think?

What would you do and say if you found out that God is the Supreme God and that He has a counsel of lower-ranking Gods? Or if His counsel is a group of angels that He runs things past or delegates to? Would it change your thinking about Him? Would it change how you worship Him? For those of you who believe that God and Jesus are the same, one incorporeal Being who came to Earth as a man and then returned to Heaven as Spirit, how would you view things differently if you discovered that this belief was false?

Do some research, explore the historical texts and commentaries, and see what the research shows. Then ask God and see what He says. Email me and let me know!

God's Image and Likeness

Christians have distorted the Genesis story of "God's image and likeness" to refer to the physical sense of the flesh. In Hebrew and Aramaic, the belief is that God's image reveals God's nature, and likeness is not confined to looks but expands to personality and nature. If God is Spirit we are Spirit. I will say there are some big hints within the story of Adam and Eve (Chavah) and Noah's story. Check out the section on "Old Testament Nakedness" to learn more.

God "Remembered"

In Hebrew, the word for remember, "zakar", means "to pay attention to". It does not mean that God had forgotten something or someone and then later remembered. It is more intimate of an action. It means that God faithfully kept His promises. When God remembers us He pays attention to us and keeps His promises.

Goddess Artemis (of Ephesians)

Artemis was the goddess of vegetation, wild animals, the hunt, chastity, and childbirth. People believed that she kept mothers safe during childbirth[9]. She was the daughter of Zeus and the twin sister of Apollo. Artemis vowed to never marry as she preferred the single life. She was also the influence that some of the early church members were fussing and fighting about that Paul had to write about [see below "Paul's Letter to Church of Corinthians"].

Human Sacrifices

I know you're wondering why I included this section in this book. It's simple, it was part of the history and needs to be included for context. Also, do you not pay homage to Jesus who was sacrificed as the "Lamb" for the sins committed against him and mankind? The human sacrifice of adults and children were normal occurrences, even if in some societies it was looked down upon. Historians and archaeologists have confirmed thousands upon thousands of cases of ritualistic sacrifice around the world, and yes, even in the ancient cities we read about in the Bible. People were sacrificed to appease the gods, human rulers, spirits, dead ancestors, or an authoritative person like a priest. Findings date back to prehistoric times. In the Bible, it is discussed in Jeremiah 7:31, 19:5, and 32:35. It is also shared in the account of Abraham taking Isaac for sacrifice [Gen. 22], and God stopped him and told him to instead sacrifice a ram. That is why there wasn't sheer outrage or defiance by Abraham when God told him to sacrifice Isaac; it's because it wasn't an uncommon practice. Also, Abraham was wise enough to know that if God said his legacy was to come from Isaac, then it couldn't be that God would have him sacrifice Isaac. We can deduce that.

This was the first time human sacrifice was mentioned in the Bible but not the last, as we know it was prohibited as a practice by the Israelites in Deuteronomy 12:31 and 18:9-12. Then in 2 Kings 3:27, King Moab sacrificed his firstborn son and heir, during a battle with the Israelites. Moab was desperate for divine intervention and made the sacrifice hoping for favor. In Judges 11, Jephthah, it is assumed, kept his word about sacrificing (as a burnt offering) whoever came out of his home, which unfortunately was his daughter. From the readings, he even gave her time to roam the hills and weep with her friends. In 2 Kings 16:3, we read about King Ahaz (king of Judah) sacrificing his son and in 2 Chronicles 33:6, we read about another king of Judah, Manasseh, sacrificing his sons, and upsetting God in the process. We now see it as murder and God forbids murder [Ex. 20:13; Deut. 5:17] but for a long time, the sacrifice was not seen as murder but rather a gift of our most precious and prized possession, in exchange for mercy and favor. How deep is that? What do we sacrifice now in hope of mercy and favor?

Idols and Idolatry

The great idols of our age are money, sex, power, and celebrities. Anything that we give more attention to and treat as equally or more important than God in our lives are things that we worship and idolize. That can be our home, car, possessions, work, and even our ministry. When we make idols they take us away from God. We have to ask ourselves, "Who is your god?" If you're consumed by thoughts of money and riches, then guess what? That is your god. We can get caught up in the fanfare of celebrities and it can grow into an obsession. You risk making them into idols. We also do this with Presidents. Look at how supporters of the 45th president of the U.S. rally around him with flags with his face on it; how they stormed the nation's Capitol at his order and encouragement. Look how many politicians praise him as though he is their savior. For many of his supporters, he is their idol. For some of them, they may have slipped far enough to make him their god, whether they know it or not. You have to ensure that you don't have idols in your heart [Ezekiel 14:7]. You can read Ezekiel 14:1-7 and see how the idolaters were condemned by God. We need to understand the importance of securing and protecting our relationship with God and how our minds place value on His creations. We're to worship the Creator not the creations.

Old Testament Nakedness

As mentioned earlier, there are some hints in the stories of Adam and Eve, and Noah, as it relates to the Hebrew word "arum" which translates to "naked" and "nakedness" and "arummim" which means "naked ones" [Gen. 2:25] but these words have a deeper meaning than nudity. Arum is derived from the verb "ur" which means "exposed". It has the meaning of "to be without something hidden"; fully transparent [Gen. 2:25]. In Genesis 9:24, the Hebrew verb is an active one, implying a purposeful action, not a passive one. And so many people translated "arum" to be "crafty" when referring to the serpent [Gen. 3:3], never considering that the serpent sheds its skin, which is transparent. Also, when you think about it, a serpent would be more "exposed" than all other animals and creatures.

Eve's name is the translation from Chavah and Adam is HaAdam (the man). They were described before the fall as having skin that was "luminous", divine light, glowing—which is how the angels were described [one example is found in Luke 2:9]. This glowing or "radiant" light is also how the face of Moses was described [Ex. 34:29-35] and Stephen's face [Acts 6:15], and how Jesus was described [Luke 9:29]. Would that not then mean that the light would also be inside of us? Maybe that is some of the glow that we see in some pregnant women; just a teeny tiny bit of that radiance from within pouring out. Maybe.

What if after the fall, not before, God covered them in flesh and not with an animal skin as many of us always thought, as the scripture says "God made" the skin and clothed them. The OJB translation of Genesis 3:21 says, "Unto Adam (man) also and to his isha (woman) did Hashem Elohim (the Name of God) make kesonos ohr (skins of light), and clothed them". So what is the hint associated with Noah? Check out the next section to learn more.

Noah

In Genesis 9:21-24, Noah made wine (this is the first mention of alcohol in the Bible) and he got sloppy drunk and passed out. It says that he was "uncovered" inside of his tent (ohel). Back in Genesis 3, God covered Adam and Eve. Now Noah is uncovered. Let's skip past contemplating which son (Ham) or grandson (Canaan) saw Noah's "erom" (nakedness) and get to verse 23 when Shem and Japheth took a garment, put it on their shoulders, walked backward, and covered the nakedness of their father. It says that their faces were turned so as not to see his nakedness. Verse 24 says that Noah awoke from his sleep (yayin) and had knowledge (da'as) of what his youngest son (ben katan) [which could also mean grandson] had done unto him. Remember, Adam and Eve's "eyes" were "opened", meaning they were made aware, and had knowledge that they were "naked". They had no clue of this before in Genesis 2:25. It was only after the serpent revealed the truth. Then they tried to cover themselves. What if Noah's drunkenness revealed his light, and that is why his sons walked backward, keeping their faces turned so they could cover him and dim the light. We read of later accounts of people being overwhelmed at the sight of the bright light. Because it can't just be their dad's nudity that has them acting like this. Do we really think that four grown men who lived together hadn't seen each other nude? That would make no sense and it definitely wouldn't explain why Noah cursed his grandson Canaan (and all of the generations that followed him) to always serve the families of Shem and Japheth. Seeing grandpa's man-parts wasn't that big of a deal back then.

So what truth, revealed, could be so significant that you couldn't risk other people knowing it? Maybe not so much as who you are but WHAT you are, could that be worthy of silence through a curse? What do you think? We will explore this with greater focus and intensity in Seek Him: Workbook 3 and most likely in another future book that I'm currently in the process of outlining.

Paul's Letter to Church of Corinth [1 Corinthians 14:26-35]

If you read Day 144 "A Woman's Place?" in Seek Him, Volume 2, then this section is picking up where we left off and digging into areas that weren't fully covered in Volume 2. Below is 1 Corinthians 14:26-35 in the Orthodox Jewish Bible translation. We are digging way deep into the controversial passages that religious leaders have perverted to support and propel a patriarchal reign over women, in a twisted way of taking the reins from God to ensure that His curse on Eve would greatly impact all women. You can compare the OJB version to the translations that are your go-to versions. Are you ready to get started? Okay let's proceed:

26 Nu? (Well?) Achim b'Moshiach (anointed brothers), when you come together, each one has a mizmor (hymn, psalm), a musar (teaching with an ethical point), a dvar hisgalus (a dvar of revelation), a lashon (tongue), or a pitron (interpretation) of a lashon (tongue); let all things be for edification.

27 If anyone speaks in a lashon (tongue), let the speakers be shenayim (two) or at most shloshah (three), and by turn, and let one give the pitron (interpretation).

28 But if there is no one to give the pitron (interpretation), let the one with the lashon (tongue) be silent in the kehillah (congregation) and let him instead speak to himself and to Hashem (The Name).

29 And let shenayim (two) or shloshah (three) nevi'im (prophets) speak and let the other nevi'im (prophets) be used with discernings of ruchot (spirits) (12:10).

30 And if a dvar hisgalus (a word of revelation) is given to a navi (prophet) sitting by, let the first navi (prophet) become silent.

31 For you all are able one by one to speak forth a dvar hanevu'ah (word of prophecy), in order that all may learn and receive chizzuk (strengthening).

32 And the neshamot (souls) of nevi'im (prophets) are subject to the nevi'im (prophets).

33 For Hashem (The Name) is no Elohei HaMevucha (the G-d of Confusion, Tohu); He is Elohei HaShalom (the God of Peace), and this is so in all the kehillot (communities) of the Kadoshim (Holy Ones).

34 Let the nashim (wives) in the kehillot (congregations) be silent, for it is not permitted for them to blurt out, but let them become submissive, as it says in the Torah (BERESHIS 3:16).

35 And if the nashim (wives) wish to inquire about something, let them inquire of their own be'alim b'bayis (husbands at home), for it is a bushah (shame) for an isha (woman) to blurt out in the kehillah (congregation) (BERESHIS 3:2).

Context of Those Times

What was going on was that during those times, the churches of Corinth were being influenced by people with self-serving motives [sound familiar?]. There was great division in the church [1 Cor. 1:10-13] with some members claiming to only be followers of Paul, or Apollos, or Peter, or Jesus [v.12], so factions were developing and it was causing a lot of grief and turmoil. It is quite reasonable to believe that they were also being influenced by the cultures of the people in their area. As the saying goes, "Birds of a feather flock together," sometimes we find ourselves assimilating within other cultures and norms and losing ourselves in the process. An example of this is that Gnosticism was being taught and practiced at Ephesus. Gnostics believe in various religious ideas and systems. There was a segment of the church that subscribed to, or at least, beginning to be greatly influenced by some of the religious beliefs of a group (or some would say a cult) that believed in the Greek goddess, Artemis, also known as Artemis of the Ephesians [see Acts 19]. Christian women prayed to her and blended worship of her with the worship of Jesus. You can read more about gnostics and Artemis in this GREATER CONTEXT chapter.

Congregants were being accused of spreading false teaching in the church about demigods and demons, Jesus, God, and about Adam and Eve— among other things. Some who also practiced goddess worship, also believed that man (Adam) came from the woman (Eve), not the other way around; believing that woman was created first. They also taught that Eve brought knowledge to humankind, which of course early Christians and Jews denounced as "what is falsely called knowledge" (1 Tim. 6:20-21) into the world.

When you read the previous passages, all congregants were told to practice decorum. During those times, they were living in exile in Greece, under Roman rule, dealing with persecution, and the early churches had small congregations that usually had their start in the homes of the congregants [Acts 18:7]. Isn't that how most churches get their start? As you grow out of homes you start finding larger structures to meet.

You can already see from previous passages, that frequent interruptions and arguments by the entire congregation had become an issue in the church, and Paul was trying to help get things in order. Verse 35, depending on which translation you read, states that if women have questions or "... if they [the women] wish 'to learn" (Greek: *mathein*) then they should ask their husbands at home. This means that the practice in the church was that women also learned with the men, and as we examined earlier, taught men and women. Women weren't excluded from learning. The issue here is either one of two things: 1) that there was a belief in learning quietly and some people were complaining that the women weren't complying with this, or 2) some people (most likely traditional Jewish men) were trying to dictate to the women how they could engage in the church.

Let's address the first possible issue: People new to the practice of silent learning would most likely interrupt the teaching with tons of questions; just like in modern times, one question can lead to a series of questions, some of which may be rudimentary. As a college professor, I deal with that regularly. It's like a domino effect. It is believed by some scholars that, unknowingly, women interrupted the teachings and did not realize they were being rude, that their behavior was culturally inappropriate. Paul's writing to the church was said to be instruction on how to deal with the unrefined women, who hadn't been molded by their customs and routines. However, it would appear from verse 38, that Paul was referring to people in general—interrupting and asking ignorant questions. And it was taboo for women to ask another woman's husband questions about the teachings. If they had questions they needed to ask their own husband, and do so after the service, when they were at home. Now, the interesting thing about this is: 1) What if they weren't married? And 2) What if their husbands or other males in their household didn't have the answers to their questions?

Idle Chatter

Something else that has been controversial was the people chose to ignore what the verses said about women engaging in idle chatter during church service. That would add greater context into what Paul was addressing specifically about women in the church. I mean, imagine idle chatter in the church [sound familiar?] Let's also consider something else, when else would women and wives have the opportunity to chat and catch up, except at church? Any other time they are at home tending to their families, in the marketplaces getting produce and supplies for their household, or working in some capacity. There wasn't leisure time for chit-chat. Except, in their minds, at church. It is said that this idle chatter brought confusion to church meetings. Don't we still see that happening now? Isn't the chatter the start of the gossiping that plague our churches? Isn't the chatter, "What's sister so-and-so wearing? She knows she shouldn't be wearing that…" or even innocently, "It's so good to see brother so-and-so back in church after recovering from surgery. God is good all the time, and all the time God is good…"

Paul was addressing decorum in these church services. He was talking about people talking aloud, blurting out comments and questions, false prophesying, and other foolishness. There is something else that demonstrates that Paul's letter was smacking the congregation with a truth backhand. Read verses 36-40, that most people fail to include while busy trying to silence women in the church:

36 Or do you think God's word originated with you Corinthians? Are you the only ones to whom it was given? **37** If you claim to be a prophet or think you are spiritual, you should recognize that what I am saying is a command from the Lord himself. **38** But if you do not recognize this, you yourself will not be recognized. **39** So, my dear brothers and sisters, be eager to prophesy, and don't forbid speaking in tongues. **40** But be sure that everything is done properly and in order.

This is further proof that Paul was repeating back what the church members had outlined in their letter, and in verses 36-38 he was calling them out. He was rebuking the very people who were trying to silence and minimize the women. He was basically asking them, "Who do you people think you are? Do you think God's word originated with you? Are you the only ones the word was given to?" And then he even called out the ones who called themselves prophets or spiritual, saying that if they truly are then they should be able to discern that his words were God's commands; and if they couldn't recognize this then God wouldn't recognize them. That is a reference back to what Jesus said about never knowing those who practiced iniquity [Luke 13:27; Matt. 7:21-27]. Paul then recaps in verses 39 and 40, to both the men and the women, to be eager to prophesy, don't prevent people from speaking in tongues, just make sure that everything is done properly and in order.

"As it says in the law" -OR- "As it says in the Law (Torah)"
Additionally, a point that irked me was that this declaration about women was supposedly mentioned in the Law. I had never read it. So I researched and researched. And guess what? The Law (Torah) does not state that women should be silent or submissive. No matter how many times and different ways someone wants to cite Genesis 3:16, Genesis 2:20-24, or Job 29:21. None of these citations say that women are to be silent, and even though some try to translate and infer them to even mean law-mandated submissiveness to men, this is not even the case. They mention playing supportive partner roles, but never silent ones. In SEEK HIM, VOLUME 3, we really dive into the wife and woman's role and position in God's eyes. Head's up, the next book won't be contradicting this one. Yet, for centuries, this foolishness of silencing and forcing women into submission, beneath men, has been peddled and pushed through Jewish, Christian, and Catholic houses of worship.

It is wrong for translators to take it upon themselves to misuse the capitalization and punctuation of words. In addition to the OJB translation, who states the "Torah", other translations also capitalize the "L" to alter the statement Paul made to instead reflect something more alarming, a reference to God's Law [see CEB, ESV, NASB, TLV, and others].[10] Some, including CEV, went a step farther and wrote, "the Law of Moses". Rather, if people had left his writing alone, as-is, and noted that Paul was talking about the rules (the law) of their congregation. Doesn't your church have by-laws that govern your congregation? Well, you can thank Paul and other leaders for providing an ancient outline, even though folks mistranslated and misunderstood a lot along the way. Paul and other leaders were redefining who they were and how they would conduct themselves as followers of Yeshua HaMashiach (Jesus the Anointed One).

This laid their personal law as defined by the New Covenant, not solely by the Old Covenant. They were breaking from traditional Jews and so a lot of things would be changed. Consider, that, through Jesus' teachings and daily walk, he was encouraging and embracing women into the ministry. Do you remember when he allowed Mary to sit at his feet while he taught? [Luke 10:38-42]. Do you remember there were numerous times where the crowd of followers and listeners included women? This wasn't widely accepted in Judaism. Yes, there were some prophetesses [see the section "Women Prophets" in this chapter], however, it was not a widely accepted practice of including and merging women into the study, teaching, and worship alongside the men until Jesus came and planted the seed that would begin rocking the boat. Read the section "Women in Judaism" to learn about women's rights, roles, and more.

Unfortunately, even though Paul and others tried to rectify, reconcile, and fix this discrepancy, we see that to this day, women's voices and roles within various churches and religious institutions have been silenced, or drastically scaled-down. Imagine Jesus walking through today's churches, cathedrals, and synagogues. Tables, pews, lecterns, and chairs would be flying everywhere. You know Jesus was a table-flipping rabbi!

Prophecies Fulfilled by Jesus

It is said that more than 100 prophecies were fulfilled by Jesus. We're not going to attempt to cover them here, but let's look at some of them:

- The nations will be blessed through Abraham's lineage [Gen. 12:3] and Jacob's offspring [Gen. 28:14] were fulfilled by Jesus in Acts 3:25-26 and Luke 3:34.
- God's covenant with Isaac's ancestors [Gen. 17:9] was fulfilled by Jesus in Romans 9:7.
- The scepter will come through Judah [Gen. 49:10] was fulfilled by Jesus in Luke 3:33.
- David's offspring will have an eternal kingdom [2 Sam. 7:12–13] was fulfilled by Jesus in Matthew 1:1.
- In Isaiah 7:14 it said that a virgin would give birth and he will be called Immanuel (God with us). This was fulfilled in Luke 1:35.
- The Messiah would end up in Egypt [Hosea 11:1] was fulfilled in Matthew 2:14-15.
- The Christ will be born in Bethlehem [Micah 5:2] was fulfilled in Matthew 2:4-6

Why do you think it was important for Jesus to fulfill the prophecies? Why was it important to him to complete everything God declared through the prophets?

Righteous/Righteousness

I decided to emphasize these words because a lot of people, myself included, can get so caught up in our heads that we think we're right and always on the right side of a situation. We can be so self-righteous that we think that God is looking at us with pride and joy in His heart, and that is a slippery slope to try to stand on since that is merely our opinion. So let's talk about righteousness and what is said in the Bible (our go-to manual and tool).

What is righteousness?

Is it something that we achieve before others? [Matt. 5:20] Or is it about us being righteous before God? [Romans 1:17] Or is it about us doing and being both?

Who determines and defines righteousness and who's righteous?

God is the paradigm and source of righteousness, the source of all values, morals, and ethics. Paul wrote of achieving righteousness in two possible ways: by adhering to the Torah (the Law of Moses) and through faith in the atonement that came from the death and resurrection of Jesus [Romans 10:3-10]. You have some people who believe that the latter is both a sufficient qualifier and the ultimate indicator of righteousness. Others say that following the Law (Torah) makes one righteous. And then you have folks that say, "you must do both" and that it is our faith and works that earn you this properly-aligned position in God's eyes.

Let's look at the men and women of the Bible who were called righteous: Noah [Gen 6:9, 7:1], Lot [2 Peter 2:8], Joseph of Arimathea [Luke 23:50], Abel [Heb 11:4; Matt 23:35; 1 John 3:12], Joseph [Matt 1:19], Cornelius [Acts 10:22], John the Baptist [Mark 6:20], Zacharius [Luke 1:5-6, Elisabeth [Luke 1:5-6], Simeon [Luke 2:25], and of course, Jesus. King Melchizedek's name means "King of Righteousness"[Gen 14:18-20; Heb 7:1-2], Daniel, Noah, and Job were said by God to have righteousness [Ez 14:14, 20]. Barak, Samson, Gideon, Jephthah, and the prophets were all said to have performed righteous acts. They all chose to be obedient. They all chose the will of God. But the only one that was sinless and perfect was and is Jesus. So who are we to point fingers and declare who is and isn't righteous? Shouldn't we be leaving that to God? Shouldn't we be walking humbly thinking that we always fall short and thereby we can never self-qualify? Are we not righteous in God and thereby only God can determine who is righteous? What do you think?

Satan: Part 2

If you read the GREATER CONTEXT chapter in SEEK HIM: Workbook 1, then you know that I provided some cultural and spiritual context on Satan, and all the names attributed to our enemy. So now, let's just add more context. Not much is told in the Bible of the origins of Satan. Hints may be found in Ezekiel 28 and a few other passages in the Bible. Behind the evil in the world stands the one [we call Satan or the devil] who blinds the minds of the unbelieving (2 Cor. 4:4). Ezekiel 28 is saying that Satan, the ruler of this world was behind the ruler of Tyre. When you read Isaiah 14:12-23 and Revelation 12 side-by-side, it seems that both humans and Satan were created good.

Ezekiel 28:12-23 says "the model of perfection, full of wisdom, and perfect in beauty. You were in Eden, the garden of God". In the OJB translation, verse 12 speaks of him that fell from the heavens, "O Heilel Ben Shachar" (Bright one of the Dawn) also translated as Day Star and Lucifer. It appears that Satan was an angel [in Arab and Muslim culture, they noted him as a Jinn, which I spoke about in SEEK HIM: Workbook 1]. In verse 14 it says that he was "...anointed as a guardian cherub, for I ordained you. You were on the holy mount of God".

Satan had access to the throne of Grace and the presence of God. Verse 15 says "He was blameless in his ways" but rather than worshiping God on the Mountain of God, "his heart became proud, going around saying, "I'm a god. I sit on God's divine throne, ruling the sea" (verse 2) because he was "trying to be a god", which is what King Tyre was guilty of. Both failed in thinking themselves wiser than the wisest, in the case of Tyre, he thought he was wiser than Daniel (verse 3). God continues by saying in verse 5 that "By your great skill in trading you have increased your wealth and because of your wealth your heart has grown proud". In verse 17 we see that Satan's heart (that he exalted to be at the level or higher than God) and corrupted wisdom is the reason God cast him out and threw him down to earth. Pride was the sin that got the best of him.

When you look at how to fight your enemy you have to study them, study their strengths and weaknesses, and look at the opportunities that you can leverage in your favor and the threats that can potentially backfire your plans. That is what Satan does with us. Yet, we don't study and strategize against him. We basically operate from the position of weakness, at his mercy—to one who does not show mercy or restraint. How ironic is that? How can you protect yourself from a threat you do not know? His weaknesses are the very things he traps us with. We're called to be in alignment with God; rebellion is Satan's way while obedience to God must be our way to salvation.

Servant

The Hebrew word for servant is "eved". This same word is used to call someone a worshiper, slave [see below], or worker. The root verb "avad" means to work or to serve. The noun form is "avodah" which, in addition to work, also means service and ministry. Now that we have those details ironed out, let's focus intently on the message. To be called a servant of God is not something to take lightly. But sadly, many of us do. We casually use the term without much thought of the responsibility and the consequences. The Oxford Dictionary defines a servant as a "devoted and helpful follower or supporter". In the Bible, God's servants (avodah) were those who worshiped Him and carried out His will. Oftentimes, these individuals had important leadership roles, but this was not always the case. Many served without being given a title.

Seven Deadly Sins

Pride, Greed, Wrath, Envy, Lust, Gluttony, and Sloth. Did you know that the seven deadly sins (also known as "Cardinal sins") are not mentioned as a list or a theme in the Bible? Don't believe me? Go flip through your Bible and come back, never, when you find them. This list of sins is contrary to the seven heavenly virtues: prudence, justice, temperance, courage (or fortitude), faith, hope, and charity [a list adopted by the ancient Christian theologians referred to as the "Church Fathers"]. The classification of the seven deadly sins was first recorded before Christianity took formal shape. Records show there were Greco-Roman predecessors, such as the Greek Philosopher, Aristotle, who listed several virtues and vices, and built upon his belief that each virtue has a desirable middle ground (called a golden mean) between two extreme vices. Aristotle listed the virtues of courage, measured anger, wit, generosity, self-control (temperance), charm, magnanimity (greatness of soul), and friendship.

The modern classification was done by early monks, hermits, and ascetics, who were called the Desert Fathers, because they lived mostly in the deserts of Egypt, in or around Scetes, in or about the third century AD. One of the monks, Evagrius Ponticus, outlined in Greek, eight evil thoughts or spirits that people were to overcome: gluttony, prostitution/fornication, avarice (greed), sadness at other's great fortune (envy), wrath, dejection, boasting, and pride. The classification was brought to Europe by his student, John Cassian, who wrote a book (in Latin) where they were translated as gluttony, lust/fornication, avarice/greed, sorrow/despair/despondency, wrath, sloth, vainglory, and pride/hubris. This list is what later became the basis for the fundamental practice of confessionals in the Catholic church.

If you ever read Dante's Purgatory, then you may recall reading about the penitents of Mount Purgatory being grouped and then penanced together based on their worst sin. Dante defines most of the sins as perverted or corrupted versions of love, except for sloth, which is a deficiency of love. The list of deadly sins has been used by the Catholic church to help their congregants from entertaining evil inclinations before they grow, fester, and consume them. Of the seven sins, pride is taught as being the worst because it severs our soul from the grace of God. This is said to be the very essence of evil as well as greed, as they underlie all other sins. Pride is the absence of humility. Pope Gregory I, revised the list in 590 AD to what we now refer to. He combined sorrow/despair/despondency with sloth, and combined vainglory with pride and hubris. Then he added to the list envy ["invidia" in Latin][11].

Slave and Slavery Examined and Compared

Those who use the Bible to condone and formalize the indefinite enslavement of people are people who won't like what God has in store for them. People completely misunderstood what a slave was in ancient times. What Europeans and others did to Africans and what American slave owners continued to do to Africans and their descendants in America, is not the slave system that God was regulating through the Torah, TaNaKh, and other sources. He was opposed to that, hence the reason He clearly articulated and defined the rules, laws, and expectations on servitude. That doesn't mean that man complied. Heck, some of the Jewish descendants of those who were enslaved in Egypt were actively involved in the African slave trade in Europe, the Americas, Brazil, and the Caribbean (especially in the latter two regions) [12].

Approximately 40% of Jews[13] (1.25% of Southern slave owners[14]) in the United States owned slaves during the Atlantic Slave Trade. Rabbis, like David Einhorn and Michael Heilprin, in the North, opposed this perverted form of slavery[15] and said that it was immoral and not endorsed by Judaism[16]. While some rabbis in the South, like Morris Jacob Raphall[17] and Isaac Leeser, supported it[18] and used the TaNaKh to support their arguments. Although Jews only made up 1.25% of southern slave owners, and this percentage was lower than what was rumored to be[19], the case remains that they took part in the African slave trade with a full understanding of what slavery meant and did to their own people. This number also does not reflect the statistics for their role in trade throughout the Atlantic triangle [mentioned earlier]. But we all know that God is Sovereign, and He will deal with everyone, Jew and non-Jew—past, present, and future— as only He can. So let's resume our talk about what ancient slavery was and wasn't so you can counter the foolish arguments that you may hear or read, that tries to pardon the sins of oppressors.

Hebrew Rules Governing Slaves

The Hebrew Bible has two sets of rules governing slaves: Hebrew slaves [Lev. 25:39-43] and Canaanite slaves [Lev. 25:45-46] who if you paid close attention to your Bible study, you know that Canaanites are of the lineage of Canaan, Ham's son and Noah's grandson. I talk more about them later in this section. All non-Hebrew slaves were mainly prisoners of war[20] Some people came as slaves, in the form of bondservants, to pay off debts or to better position themselves financially (as they earned wages and were released with food and animals) at the end of their sentence. These slaves served only six years and under certain conditions (like serious injury) could be released sooner. There were instances when, if those conditions weren't met, an owner could keep a non-Jewish slave indefinitely. This is the loophole that slavers of Africans used to support their tactics.

Sometimes impoverished families would sell their children and other family members as slaves. They needed the money and someone had to be sacrificed temporarily. Joseph's brothers sold him to the Midianites [the lineage of Abraham's son Midian, whose mother was Keturah]. They then handed him over to Potiphar [Pharoah's official and commander of the bodyguard]. Joseph's brothers didn't need the money, as they were wealthy. They were just being greedy, spiteful, and trying to find a way to cover up what they had done to him. I'm sure with Jacob/Israel being older, the sons assumed that by the time Joseph worked off his time in slavery, their father would be deceased, and they would be free from the guilt of their crime. They had no clue that God's plans were already in motion and couldn't be stopped.

Leviticus 25:47-51 says that Jewish slaves owned by non-Jews could be redeemed (have their freedom purchased). Of course, this rule was perverted and used against them by non-Jews who started ransoming the Jewish slaves for exorbitant prices[21], knowing the Jewish custom of redemption of captives would mean that even if the slave came from a poor family, the Jewish collective would raise the funds for the freedom of the slave.[22] African slaves were never allowed to be redeemed by their families, because they were kidnapped and sold as property (not indentured or paid servants) and shipped thousands of miles away from their homes, most to never see their families or freedom again. They weren't prisoners of war. They were sacrificial lambs of convenience. Easily disposable. If people don't atone for their ancestors' actions and the privileges (and inheritances) that they have received from these actions, they will have to answer to a God that won't look favorably on the complete disregard and absolute rebellion against Him.

Treatment of Slaves

According to the traditional Jewish law, a slave was to be more like an indentured servant, where the person takes out a loan and works it off (through free labor) for a specific period. This was also common practice to pay your way to a new city, town, or country. They were passengers, not property. This servant had rights and was to be treated almost like a member of the owner's family. Look back through the Old Testament, look at how Abraham, Isaac, and Jacob treated their slaves. Do you remember when Abraham sent Eliezer to find Isaac a bride? There weren't any slave catchers riding around rounding up slaves who weren't with their master, and he didn't have to carry a written permission slip (that could still be ignored). Now of course this is not to say that there wasn't mistreatment of Hebrew and non-Hebrew slaves. But those weren't done by people following the rules and laws of God. Those were people led by Satan (whether they want to admit to it or not).

Do you remember when Jacob was a slave to his uncle, Laban, for 20 years? He was an indentured servant who wanted to marry Laban's younger daughter, Rachel, so he offered to work seven years in exchange for her [Genesis 29:18]. Now, as the story reflects, Laban was a greedy booger (and filled with pride) and he locked Jacob in for an additional seven-year agreement [Gen. 29:27-28] as bridal payment (due to Laban's switcheroo with the daughters)[23], and then the third time lasted six years so that Jacob could help increase Laban's flocks and cattle, and leave with a portion for his own family [Gen. 30:32-33]. Jacob realized that Laban wasn't about to let him go at the end of this sixth year, so he obeyed God and left. He had more than satisfied his service agreement. They eventually formed a covenant to formally resolve things. What slavery was and what it evolved into through perversion, are two different spheres. It was to be that they were treated as part of the fold, part of the family, indistinguishable— not as commodities.

Maimonides wrote (Yad, Avadim 9:8)[24] that it didn't matter if a slave was Jewish or not, "*The way of the pious and the wise is to be compassionate and to pursue justice, not to overburden or oppress a slave, and to provide them from every dish and every drink. The early sages would give their slaves from every dish on their table. They would feed their servants before sitting to their own meals ... Slaves may not be maltreated or offended — the law destined them for service, not for humiliation. Do not shout at them or be angry with them, but hear them out*". In another context, he wrote that all the laws of slavery are "*mercy, compassion and forbearance*"[25] which we never saw in the American slave trade. We don't even see this in most households that have live-in servants.

Sex and Marriage With Slaves

Classical rabbis also forbade masters from marrying their female slaves. The Torah says that an owner cannot have sex with an engaged slave [Lev. 19:20-22] and we already know how God feels about adultery, so there is no way that you could have sex with a married slave, and nowhere no way can you rape and think it's somehow acceptable.

"They're Not Human" Argument

These were the words and sentiments of slave owners in the Americas and elsewhere. They said that Africans weren't human. Even when they raped and had children with the women, they continued to proclaim that African people were not human. Even when these slaves served as nursemaids, breastfeeding and taking care of white babies, the slaves weren't considered as human. It was said that they didn't have souls like the Europeans, Arabs, Jews, and others who were trading them like bags of salt or stacks of lumber. Africans were treated as and worse than animals. They were tagged and branded like animals. All of this was said and done by slave owners to counter-argue any Biblical or other religious text that denounced slavery and the slave trade. By dehumanizing Africans, they could justify the mistreatment of them. They could rape, beat, torture, starve, lynch, and murder them, simply because they could—because Black people had no rights. I bet those farm animals they had to care for had rights though—which is why today's animal rights activists need to stop comparing the exploitation of animals to chattel slavery of humans [please and thank you].

We still see those dehumanizing tactics used today, they are just more refined, polished, and covert than their ancestors. But don't ever be confused by "who" they are serving, and know that it was not and is not the God of Noah, Abraham, Isaac, Jacob, Joseph, Mary, or Jesus. Don't be fooled, Satan's hands are all over this, but God will prevail.

Curse of Ham Argument

For those who use Noah's curse upon Ham's line through Canaan [Gen. 9:25-27] as justification for slavery, people aren't paying close attention that Canaanites could leverage their lineage just as Jewish women could, by performing certain mitzvot (commandments by God) giving them higher rank that gentiles and even sparing their lives. Also, Canaanite slaves could be emancipated and through this emancipation, they were "freeborn" and made part of the Jewish fold, and allowed to marry a daughter of Israel[26]. They were also expected to be elevated in status at some point. These rules were also used in general to refer to any non-Hebrew slave [Lev. 25:45-46]. That was not the life of the African slave nor the descendants of Africans born in the Americas as slaves. It was said, as a default argument, that Canaan's line were Africans or cursed to be dark-skinned, and that curse meant a lifetime of slavery. But race nor skin color were ever mentioned in the Bible and Canaanites were not the singular lineage to define Africans. How could one line spread and populate an entire continent, and be so divided and different at the same time?

Besides, look closely at Ham's other sons names and the nations that were grew and rose from their lineage: Cush [Ethiopia], Mizraim [Egypt], Put [Libya]. Cush's son Nimrod had several kingdoms including Babel (the Hebrew name for Babylon), as in the same place where the Tower of Babel was erected, and the same group of people who held the nation of Israel in captivity. But Noah didn't curse Ham or Ham's other sons, just Canaan. Honestly, some folks reached far and wide using the Bible to justify enslaving Africans. Even if you want to ignorantly claim that all African people are Canaanites, you still would need to go back to the laws that stated that Canaanites could leverage their lineage, which means they could be at a rank higher than their captors. If that was and is the case, then there is more than reparations due to African people in the Americas and Europe. Noah's curse on Canaan ensured that Shem's line would be guaranteed Canaan's land, as proclaimed later by God to Abraham, Isaac, and Jacob. What land did Jacob/Israel's people eventually inhabit? Canaan's land. Yes, and what does archaeological evidence show? Early Israelites were in fact Canaanites. So where does that leave things?

Irish Were Slaves Too?!?

This has been a widely circulated myth on social media, especially Facebook. Let's clear this up. The Irish were indentured servants, not chattel slaves. Yes, many were subjected to forced labor, but most were not. They served four to seven years as bondservants. There were restrictions on marriage, pregnancy, and travel. Those who were shipped away from Ireland (after the brutal conquest of Ireland led by England's Oliver Cromwell] had service periods of usually five to seven years, before 1661. In 1661, a new law was passed that Irish bondservants in Barbados only had to serve two to four years. This was done to entice the Irish to migrate to the colonies, and it was used to single them out when they weren't needed. In 1655 tough laws were imposed on Irish servants who arrived in Virginia but they weren't indentured. Their penalty was two years longer than Christian servants and three years longer for those under the age of 16. This law was repealed in 1660.

My great great great grandfather was of Irish descent. I don't know if he came to this country as an indentured servant or as a free man, but if the former, I know he only served for no more than seven years, and then was free to live his life and take part in this new world. Unlike my great great great grandmother who didn't have those privileges. Make sense? So let's stop trying to dilute the African slave experience with the Irish one. Thank you.

In Conclusion

This is just some of the information that sets apart ancient slavery from the savagery that we saw enforced upon African people for 247 years, followed by 100 years of Black codes, sharecropping, and Jim Crow, and in our more recent times—56 years of mass incarceration, all of which is the aftermath and continuation of reconstructed enslavement of a people. There has been no redemption, restoration, or reparations. Why? Because you still have people who believe that this past and present mistreatment is justified as part of Canaan being cursed, and ignorantly confusing or conflating Canaan with his father Ham, and clumping in all of Ham's children (as the only other way to further justify this mixup). The mass incarceration of Black people and the careless disregard of taking a Black life, is all justified because some uninformed people keep miquoting the Bible, believing that Black lives don't actually matter because those lives have been cursed. This foolishness alone is deserving of recompense. The German government has paid out more than $80 Billion in Holocaust reparations since 1952 and they are paying $662 million to Holocaust survivors (about 240,000 people) struggling because of the COVID-19 pandemic[27]. When you know you're wrong and that you have done wrong, you own up to it, take full responsibility, repent, and you don't continue causing harm. The Americas and Europe have a long way to go to make things right. Hopefully, they will. For their souls' sake.

Spirit and Soul

I wanted to give you a visual of something to consider how we navigate through life with our spirit and soul. Are you ready?

Visualize an outline of the human body and within that outer layer, two inner silhouettes have the same outline. The outer layer is the body itself. The skin and flesh. God gave us a body, and in ancient times many people referred to it as a tent. Many people today call it a shell, a vessel, a house. I believe this body makes it possible for us to make our way around this planet and it gives us a common appearance and characterization that differs from all other creatures, domestic and foreign ("alien"). The body stores and carries around organs, cells, and fluids that work synergistically. The body has receptors that allow us to feel and we express our feelings through the soul. That is the second inner layer.

The soul is how we were defined in ancient times. We weren't casually referred to as humans but rather souls. The third inner layer is the spirit. It's our direct connection to God. When we speak in the spirit we speak in our natural essence. It is our communication portal.

Our soul expresses through the spirit our humanness and at the same time, it allows us to express fully all that is of God. It is the one thing that angels lack. They can walk amongst us in these shells called bodies. They too are spiritual beings. But the thing that made some of them revolt against us is the envy from not having the special feature called a soul. Yes, our soul makes us highly emotional creatures and when not harnessed properly we can be destructive. But imagine your life without it. Imagine not being able to express empathy and compassion. Imagine not cooing over babies. Imagine not having a sense of humor. And to read my books and spend time with me, you need a sense of humor! Did I make you giggle a little just now? I hope so.

Walk/Walking With God

Of all of the Biblical accounts, only three men are said to have "walked with God": Enoch, Noah, and Levi. Read Genesis 5 and Genesis 6, and Malachi 2. To walk with God is to be in fellowship with Him, talking, acting, looking, and living like Him. That is the true representation of being in His image and likeness. The book of Colossians says that Jesus is the "expressed image of God", made in His image, just as we are. When you see Jesus you see God. That is what our goal is— to walk each day expressing Him, being fully in His image, so that when people see and speak to us they see and hear Him.

Enoch is the first man recorded to live as long as 365 years (of that number is accurate) and unlike the other men of the Bible, he didn't die, he ascended. Look back through the history of the line. Adam, Seth, Enosh, Kenan, Mahalel, and Jared all "lived, fathered children, then died". When you get to Enoch it says he lived, fathered Methuselah, walked with God continually for 300 years, fathered more children, and continued to walk with God. It doesn't say that he then died. Nope, it says, "then he was not there, because God took him". When you look at Methuselah, Lamech (Noah's dad), and then Noah, they all lived, fathered, and died.

In the book of Matthew, he writes of Jesus saying that we're to walk humbly with God and that to do so is to live in such a way that when other people see the good that you do they will glorify God who is in Heaven (Matt. 5:16). That is supposed to be all of our goals.

Who do people see when they encounter you?

Women Leaders in Judaism, Christianity & Catholicism

Female Deacons

In Romans 16:1-2, Paul writes a letter commending a female deaconess of the church in Cenchreae [SEHN-kree-ay]. Her name was sister Phoebe. She is the person who delivered Paul's letter to the congregation. Paul wrote, "*So you should welcome her in the Lord in a manner worthy of the saints and assist her in whatever matter she may require your help. For indeed she has been a benefactor of many—and of me also. I commend to you our sister Phoebe, who is a servant of the church in Cenchreae."* A benefactor is a helper of a person or a cause. Phoebe was called Sister Phoebe. By giving her the name "Sister", this also signifies her status as a Christian. She's a member of a spiritual family. It's not a title given to all women. The word for "servant" in Greek (as this is translated from Greek) is diakonos [dee-ak'-on-os]. In English that word is translated as "deacon" or "deaconess" (when spoken in the feminine). If you're surprised that there were female deacons, then your mind is probably spinning to know they also served as bishops and priests.

Christian Churches Stance

There are approximately 15 historical records of ordained women in antiquity. Although the Catholic and Orthodox Churches claim that those ordinations were by heretical groups and don't count. They stated that ordaining female priests and bishops is unacceptable in the Church. For only a baptized man can validly receive sacred ordination as a matter of divine law. This has been reinforced as of 2014 by Pope Francis who said this is a non-issue. Then January 2021 he "changed" Vatican law to allow women to do more as laypersons during Mass[28]. They still aren't allowed to hold positions as deacons, bishops, and other ordained titles. But they can read at Mass. Yes, you read that correctly. I'm citing an AP News article where Pope Francis is quoted as saying that he is creating a second commission of so-called experts to study whether women could be deacons after the first commission reported on the history of women as deacons in the early church.

Yep, darn that Paul for writing those letters and mentioning his fellow sisters in Christ who he called his equals. And in 2 John we read about John's high view of women in leadership. Who in the tarnation is paying attention to this? Obviously, the Catholic Church and some other denominations didn't think anyone was. Yes, we have seen decades of push-back from the Southern Baptist Convention and evangelical Christian leaders also limiting the role of women in the church. They all want to cite a part of a verse or two, and take them out of context to serve their biased views. Soooooo now there needs to be a second commission by the Catholic Church to either corroborate what the first commission said and what we have all read countless times, or dispute what we all know to be true. Either way and I'm sorry if my cynicism is steering through like a steamroller, but I don't see the Catholic Church backing off their long-held position to start embracing Paul and even John's mindset—that by the way, was influenced by Jesus—who clearly had women as part of his ministry. Let's pray for God's intervention to help these religious leaders get it together.

Women Prophets in the Bible

Women were called prophets or prophetesses, but the scripture makes clear that a prophetess is a female prophet who is no different than her male counterpart. The distinction between navi (prophet) and neviah (female prophet) is the feminine noun that signifies that the reference is to a woman and not a man. Below are some of the female prophets that we have recorded in the Bible, but it is not exhaustive, and does not include any possible mentions in the missing books of the Bible:

Old Testament [Old Covenant]

- Miriam—the sister of Moses [Ex. 15:20; Num. 12:2]
- Deborah—the warrior and judge [Judges 4:4-6]
- Huldah—during the reign of King Josiah [2 Kings 22:14-15; 2 Chron. 34:22]
- Noadiah—Nehemiah's nemesis [Neh. 6:14]
- Isaiah's wife was not mentioned by name, just said to be "the prophetess" [Isaiah 8:3][29]

New Testament [New Covenant]

- Anna [Luke 2:36-38; Acts 1:14; Acts 2:17]
- Philip's daughters [Acts 21:9]
- Women prophesying in church [1 Corinthians]
- Woman prophet in the Church of Thyatira that criticized by Jesus [Rev. 2:18-29]

Next Steps

Can you believe it, you have completed this workbook. I hope that you found it as a beneficial companion to Seek Him, Volume 2. I hope that it challenged you enough to push through those barriers that have been holding you back, keeping you down. You can proceed to Seek Him, Volume 3: Don't Turn Back and the companion workbook, Seek Him: Workbook 3. Or you work your way back through Volume 2 and Workbook 2 one more time. You may still have some things to work on. I get it. Although I wrote these books, I invest time each day reading, studying, and completing the activities within these books. There are some days where I struggle because I feel challenged and vulnerable. But I've grown to realize that those are the days I'm really supposed to be celebrating, because I'm being molded, and that is always an awesome experience.

That is verification that God has some big things planned for us and He needs us to be in tip-top shape to deal with the next-level things. So don't get down on yourself if you're not quite ready to dive into Volume 3. There's no guilt or shame. God meets us where we are, so just have a sit-down with Him and then go from there. If you're ready for Volume 3, I can't wait to explore these next four months with you. Soon it will be an entire year since we started this journey together. You have broken out of your comfort zone and now we're going to keep pressing forward. We won't be like Lot's wife, looking back, wondering what once was, or trying to pick up junk we need to leave behind. Let's finish this year strong, confident, and totally reliant upon God and His leadership. You can find details in the back of this book about where to get Volume 3 and Workbook 3.

I will see you soon!

NOTES

1. ^ "The Return of Hagar", commentary on Parshah Chayei Sarah, Chabad Lubavitch. https://www.chabad.org/parshah/article_cdo/aid/2636/jewish/The-Return-of-Hagar.htm
2. ^ "Parshat Chayei Sarah". Torah Insights, Orthodox Union, 2002. Web Archive. https://web.archive.org/web/20081113015839/http://www.ou.org/torah/ti/5763/chayeisara63.htm
3. ^ Angel of the Lord https://www.biblestudytools.com/dictionaries/bakers-evangelical-dictionary/angel-of-the-lord.html
4. ^ Ben Witherington, The Living Word of God (Baylor University Press 2007 ISBN 978-1-60258-017-6), p. 224. Excerpt here: https://books.google.com/books?id=xEvXKTG9Mf4C&pg=PA224#v=onepage&q&f=false
5. ^ Pew Forum on Religion and Public Life (Dec 19, 2011). Global Christianity- A Report on the Size and Distribution of the World's Christian Population. https://web.archive.org/web/20130730062627/http://www.pewforum.org/christian/global-christianity-exec.aspx
6. ^ History of Christmas. October 27, 2009. Updated December 22, 2020. https://www.history.com/topics/christmas/history-of-christmas
7. ^ Easter Symbols and Traditions. October 27, 2009. Updated April 9, 2020. https://www.history.com/topics/holidays/easter-symbols
8. ^ Magris, Aldo (2005), "Gnosticism: Gnosticism from its origins to the Middle Ages (further considerations)", in Jones, Lindsay (ed.), *MacMillan Encyclopedia of Religion*, MacMillan
9. ^ Hinkley, Chesna. (13, Feb 2019) What to Say When Someone Says Women Are Not Permitted to Teach
https://www.cbeinternational.org/resource/article/mutuality-blog-magazine/what-say-when-someone-says-women-are-not-permitted-teach
10. ^ Miller, Jeff (4, Dec. 2017). Translation Troubles: 1 Corinthians as a Test Case https://www.cbeinternational.org/resource/article/mutuality-blog-magazine/translation-troubles-1-corinthians-14-test-case
11. ^ DelCogliano, Mark (18 November 2014). Gregory the Great: Moral Reflections on the Book of Job, Volume 1. Cistercian Publications. ISBN 9780879071493.
12. ^ The Columbia History of Jews and Judaism in America, p. 43, by Rabbi Marc Lee Raphael, (Columbia University Press, February 12, 2008); ISBN 978-0231132220.
13. ^ "Total Jewish Population in the United States". www.jewishvirtuallibrary.org.

NOTES

14. ^ Rodriguez, Junius. The Historical encyclopedia of world slavery, Volume 1, ABC-CLIO, 1997
15. ^ Friedman, Murray (2007). What went wrong?: the creation and collapse of the Black-Jewish Alliance. Simon and Schuster. pp. 25–26.
16. ^ Adams, Maurianne (1999). Strangers & neighbors: relations between Blacks & Jews in the United States. University of Massachusetts Press. pp. 190–94. ISBN 1-55849-236-4..
17. ^ Benjamin, Judah, p. "Slavery and the Civil War: Part II", United States Jewry, 1776-1985: The Germanic Period, by Jacob Rader Marcus (Ed.), Wayne State University Press, 1993, pp. 17-19.
18. ^ Hertzberg, Arthur (1998). The Jews in America: four centuries of an uneasy encounter: a history. Columbia University Press. pp. 111–113. ISBN 0-231-10841-9.
19. ^ The Columbia History of Jews and Judaism in America, p. 43, by Rabbi Marc Lee Raphael, (Columbia University Press, February 12, 2008); ISBN 978-0231132220.
20. ^ Hezser, Catherine, Jewish slavery in antiquity, Oxford University Press, 2005.
21. ^ Ransoming Captive Jews. An important commandment calls for the redemption of Jewish prisoners, but how far should this mitzvah be taken? Archived at https://web.archive.org/web/20070927184438/http://www.myjewishlearning.com/daily_life/GemilutHasadim/Social_Welfare/PidyonShvuyim.htm
22. ^ Paul Johnson: A History of the Jews. 1987. p.240
23. ^ Genesis 29:21-23
24. ^ https://www.chabad.org/library/article_cdo/aid/1363819/jewish/Chapter-Nine.htm
25. ^ Encyclopedia Judaica, 2007, vol. 18, p. 670
26. ^ Jewish Encyclopedia, s.v. Slaves and Slavery https://www.jewishencyclopedia.com/articles/13799-slaves-and-slavery
27. ^ Gross, Elana Lynn (14 October 2020) "Germany Will Pay $662 Million To Holocaust Survivors Struggling Because Of The Pandemic" https://www.forbes.com/sites/elanagross/2020/10/14/germany-will-pay-662-million-to-holocaust-survivors-struggling-because-of-the-pandemic/?sh=13f039371e65
28. ^ Winfield, N. (11, January 2021). "Pope says women can read at mass, but still can't be priests". AP News. https://apnews.com/article/pope-francis-women-still-cant-be-priest-3bdcad94325be16ee2993f61eb17c5a0
29. ^ Rollston, Christopher (6 Jan 2017). "Women Prophets in the Bible: Remembering the Oft Forgotten" https://www.huffpost.com/entry/women-prophets-in-the-bib_b_8918650

ABOUT THE AUTHOR

Natasha L. Foreman is a consultant, professor, blogger, podcaster, and the author of the SEEK HIM book series. A Southern California native, yet she is a global citizen. Since 2009, she has been sharing her spiritual journey and God's love through her blog, BreakingBreadWithNatasha.com. She is a servant leader and follower of Christ, who boldly shares her stories, testimonies, and love for her Creator. For Natasha, the purpose of her service in this world is to glorify God, and she prays that each person who reads her writings feels her love for, commitment to, and faith in God.

Connect with Natasha through any of these sources:
http://twitter.com/breakbread365
http://facebook.com/breakingbreadwithnatasha
http://natashaforeman.com
http://breakingbreadwithnatasha.com

Visit D.O.M.E. Life Publishing to purchase other books written by Natasha, to sign up for our newsletter, and to stay in the loop about our newest book releases, events, and more:http://domelifepublishing.com

www.ingramcontent.com/pod-product-compliance
Lightning Source LLC
Chambersburg PA
CBHW081153070526
44583CB00021B/2825